HowExper Denver, Colorado

MW01491647

101+ Tips to Learn about the Best Places to Eat, Drink, and Explore in the Mile High City

HowExpert with Todd Faulk

For more tips related to this topic, visit HowExpert.com/denver.

Recommended Resources

- HowExpert.com –How To Guides by Everyday Experts.
- HowExpert.com/free – Free HowExpert Email Newsletter.
- HowExpert.com/books – HowExpert Books
- HowExpert.com/courses – HowExpert Courses
- HowExpert.com/clothing – HowExpert Clothing
- HowExpert.com/membership – HowExpert Membership Site
- HowExpert.com/affiliates – HowExpert Affiliate Program
- HowExpert.com/jobs – HowExpert Jobs
- HowExpert.com/writers – Write About Your #1 Passion/Knowledge/Expertise & Become a HowExpert Author.
- HowExpert.com/resources – Additional HowExpert Recommended Resources
- YouTube.com/HowExpert – Subscribe to HowExpert YouTube.
- Instagram.com/HowExpert – Follow HowExpert on Instagram.
- Facebook.com/HowExpert – Follow HowExpert on Facebook.

TikTok.com/@HowExpert – Follow HowExpert on TikTok.

Publisher's Foreword

Dear HowExpert Reader,

HowExpert publishes quick 'how to' guides on all topics from A to Z by everyday experts.

At HowExpert, our mission is to discover, empower, and maximize everyday people's talents to ultimately make a positive impact in the world for all topics from A to Z...one everyday expert at a time!

All of our HowExpert guides are written by everyday people just like you and me, who have a passion, knowledge, and expertise for a specific topic.

We take great pride in selecting everyday experts who have a passion, real-life experience in a topic, and excellent writing skills to teach you about the topic you are also passionate about and eager to learn.

We hope you get a lot of value from our HowExpert guides, and it can make a positive impact on your life in some way. All of our readers, including you, help us continue living our mission of positively impacting the world for all spheres of influences from A to Z.

If you enjoyed one of our HowExpert guides, then please take a moment to send us your feedback from wherever you got this book.

Thank you, and we wish you all the best in all aspects of life.

Sincerely,

BJ Min
Founder & Publisher of HowExpert
HowExpert.com

PS...If you are also interested in becoming a HowExpert author, then please visit our website at HowExpert.com/writers. Thank you & again, all the best!

Table of Contents

Introduction to the Mile High City

Growing up in Denver in the 1970s and 1980s, my hometown had a reputation as a "cow town." Elementary school field trips took us to the National Western Stock Show, with its cattle auctions and 4-H exhibits. Dinners out meant dressing up in cowboy hats and cowboy boots, and steak was the main thing on the menu. The downtown sidewalks were "rolled up" at 5 o'clock, and tumbleweeds actually blew down the streets on weekends. Then came the collapse of oil prices in the mid-1980s, and Denver's oil-based economy started to shrivel. People moved to the suburbs in droves, and Denver seemed like a city in permanent decline.

How things have changed three decades later. Major public investments in the 1990s, such as a huge new airport, a city-wide light rail system, and world-class art facilities, were the seeds for a major transformation of Denver that continues today. Denver has always been a frontier city, but today Denver is known for being on the frontier of the microbrewery boom, legalized marijuana, and the high-tech industry. As a result, most residents no longer consider Denver a "cowtown," although you can still find its western roots if you know where to look (this guide will help you find them). Instead, Denver is a vibrant and rapidly growing urban center known for its outdoor lifestyle, sophisticated dining scene, and high quality of life. All these qualities make Denver a highly sought-after place to live and a vacation destination in its own right.

Denver, founded in 1858 at the edge of the High Plains and at the foot of the Rocky Mountains (not in the mountains, as some easterners believe), has always been a gateway to the rest of Colorado and the Rocky Mountain region. Gold miners, hoping to strike it rich in the mountains west of town, stopped in the new boomtown to load up on supplies and get rowdy in the local saloons. Today, skiers on their way to the slopes fly into Denver, and summer road trippers stop here before heading into the mountains—not for mining, but golf or hiking.

But Denver has long *attracted* people from the rest of the region and the country. As Colorado grew, so did Denver. After its founding, the frontier outpost soon became Colorado's capital, largest city, and financial and transportation center. Eager to support the gold and silver industries, Easterners poured into Denver in the mid- and late-19th centuries, and many became wealthy. During World War II, the city, far from any coast or potential enemy attacks, became a magnet for military and federal government installations. The metro area attracted the largest number of federal agencies outside of Washington, DC. Oil production in eastern Colorado took off after the war, and Denver became a major hub for the oil industry. Remember the popular TV show *Dynasty* in the early 1980s? The show depicted Denver's oil barons, not always in a positive light. (I still think the oil family on TV's *Dallas* was more ruthless!)

Today, Denver draws a diverse range of people from all walks of life. Many come for access to the outdoors. Parks, trails, bike paths, and lakes abound in the city itself. The mountains of the Front Range—less than an hour's drive away—offer world-class skiing, hiking, rock-climbing, camping, wildlife viewing, hunting, fishing, and national parks. When in Denver, many people discover the thriving arts and music scene, numerous great restaurants and microbreweries, friendly people, and abundant sunshine, and they opt to stay. Once you get used to the high elevation—5280 feet, or one mile above sea level—you just might want to call the Mile High City home, too.

Tip #1: If you ever find yourself lost in Denver, just look for the mountains, usually visible from almost anywhere in the metro area. When you find them, you'll know you're looking west!

Chapter 1: How to Experience the Best of Denver in a Day

Overview

If you're one of the many people passing through Denver on the way to the mountains or points farther west, you might find yourself with an extra day to spend in Denver. Of course, you really need more than a day to experience all the things Denver has to offer, but if you really have only a day, you can hit some of Denver's best highlights and get a good sense of the city by following this chapter.

Most of the main attractions in the Denver area are either right downtown or within a 20-minute drive of downtown. You don't need a car for the one-day attractions because they're easily walkable from the free 16th Street Mall shuttle. The 16th Street Mall is the mile-long pedestrian zone in the heart of downtown, which is discussed more below.

Tip #2: The streets of downtown, where the city was founded, were aligned to face the South Platte River and Cherry Creek, so they are diagonal to the points of the compass.

In other words, the north-south streets actually point northwest and southeast. However, as the city grew, planners decided to fix new streets to a grid aligning with the points of the compass. As a result, it can be a little confusing where the grid boundaries come together along North Broadway and Colfax Avenue. Just pay close attention to the signs when crossing from one grid to the other to avoid getting disoriented.

Tip #3: To get the most out of a brief visit to Denver, I recommend staying in a hotel in the Upper Downtown area, which is central to most attractions.

You won't have to spend a lot of time getting from one place to the next or risk getting stuck in the infamous traffic jams on I-25, the main north-south corridor that runs the length of Metro Denver. If you feel like splurging, I recommend the historic and beautiful Brown Palace Hotel (321 17th St.), which is an attraction in itself. Less expensive options include the Homewood Suites by Hilton (550 15th St.) and the Holiday Inn Express (1715 Tremont Pl.), both within a block of the 16th Street Mall.

Essential Things to Do in Central Denver

One Mile High: The State Capitol

200 E. Colfax Ave., Denver

One of my most memorable field trips as a kid was visiting the grand State Capitol Building at the east end of Civic Center Park. Looking up to the top of the dome from inside the giant rotunda made quite an impression on me, and it still does. Sitting atop a small hill and opened in 1894, the neoclassical structure was inspired by the national Capitol Building in Washington, D.C., and was meant to dominate the Denver skyline. It long did until skyscrapers began sprouting along nearby 17th Street in the 1950s.

The State Capitol was designed to be symbolic of Colorado. Its walls are made of Colorado gray granite, and the interior is adorned with a rare rose onyx marble that was also mined in Colorado. The dome, covered in real gold leaf, is the building's most distinctive feature and commemorates the 1858-59 gold rush that gave birth to Colorado.

Getting There: Make the State Capitol your first stop of the day. Take the free 16th Street Mall shuttle to its terminus at Civic Center Station on North Broadway and walk one block south to Colfax Avenue; from here, you can't miss the imposing building. Plan to arrive for the first one-hour guided tour at 10 am; a maximum of 15 people per tour are permitted on a first-come, first-served basis. Check the tour website at https://leg.colorado.gov/content/tour-information for the latest information.

Tip #4: Walk up the Capitol's west steps and look for an engraving on the 13th step that says "One Mile Above Sea Level."

This point, exactly 5,280 feet above sea level, is where you want to take your selfie. If you see any engravings with the same moniker on the 15th and 18th steps, know that these were previously found to be inaccurate!

The Unsinkable Spirit of Denver: Molly Brown House

1340 Pennsylvania St., Denver

The Molly Brown House Museum is the best place to learn about Denver's most famous resident, the "Unsinkable Molly Brown." The Molly Brown House is the beautiful 1889 Victorian mansion where Margaret Brown (as she was known in her time) lived most of her adult life. Molly Brown is best known for surviving the sinking of the RMS *Titanic* in 1912 and encouraging a lifeboat captain to return to the wreckage for survivors. (Remember the James Cameron film *Titanic*? Molly Brown was memorably portrayed by Kathy Bates.)

Molly Brown was much more than a survivor, however. She met and married James J. Brown in Leadville, CO, and after James struck it rich in the silver mines, the couple moved to Denver (the Brown Palace is named after Henry C. Brown, not Molly's husband, as is often assumed). Molly became a philanthropist and activist and used her wealth to promote women's and workers' rights. She also was awarded the French Legion of Honor for her tireless assistance to those devastated by World War I in France.

Getting There: After exiting the State Capitol, walk south to 14th Avenue and turn left. Then walk two blocks to Pennsylvania Street and turn right; the Molly Brown House is halfway down the block on the left. You'll have time to get the last one-hour guided tour that starts at noon. If you arrive after noon, you can still take a self-guided tour until 3 pm. Note that admission to the house is limited to 12 people at a time. For the latest visitor information, visit https://mollybrown.org/visit-us/.

Tip #5: If you arrive directly from the Capitol, you will likely have some time before your noon tour.

Use that time to peruse the small but excellent museum located on the lower level of the Molly Brown House. You'll learn all about Molly Brown's fascinating life and get a good grounding for the guided tour.

The Heart of the City: The 16th Street Mall

Along 16th St. from Wewatta St. to N. Broadway, Denver

I remember when the pedestrian 16th Street Mall seemed like a novelty when it opened in 1982. In fact, it was a novelty when many cities were closing their pedestrian zones in favor of indoor shopping malls. Designed by the famed architect I.M. Pei, Denver's 16th Street Mall is still one of the largest of its kind in the United States. It can be argued that the 16th Street Mall marked the beginning of Denver's urban renewal spurring redevelopment all along its path.

At 1.25 miles long, the Mall runs the length of downtown. It is lined with dozens of busy restaurants, eateries, shops, hotels, and notable attractions like the Pavilions Shopping Mall, the Paramount Theater, Daniels & Fisher Tower, Skyline Park, and Union Station.

Not only is the Mall a major commercial magnet, but it is also an important corridor linking Lower Downtown (LoDo) with Upper Downtown and Civic Center. The MallRide—the free shuttle that runs every few minutes and stops at every block along the Mall—is used by thousands of office workers and shoppers every day. When I was in college, I used the MallRide to get from my classes at the Auraria Campus to my part-time job in the Republic Plaza building. It sure saved me a lot of money and time walking!

Getting There: After finishing your tour of the Molly Brown House, you'll probably be ready for lunch. I recommend walking back to Civic Center Station and catching the MallRide on the 16th Street Mall, which is lined with many great restaurants and eateries.

Tip #6: For a great taste of the Old West, take the MallRide to Glenarm Place and stop at West of Surrender, an old-fashioned, saloon-style restaurant, and bar. Get the Rodeo BBQ burger and choose from one of the many locally brewed draft beers. It's my favorite restaurant on the Mall.

Tip #7: After lunch, stroll north along the Mall's wide sidewalks to check out the many shops and other pedestrians, but avoid stepping off the curb and into the path of a shuttle bus! At Curtis Street, stop to gaze up at the iconic Daniels & Fisher Tower, one of Denver's oldest landmarks. This is also an excellent spot to get a selfie!

Discover Lower Downtown (LoDo)

Many newcomers to Denver think of Lower Downtown as the heart of downtown. With its gleaming new buildings, buzzy restaurants, and thriving nightlife, it's easy to see why. I guess calling it "LoDo" gives it some added cache, too. But when I was going to college at the nearby Auraria Campus in the late 1980s, Lower Downtown was a place to be avoided. It was dark and empty at night and often regarded as "skid row." It was a shame because this is where Denver began.

Today, LoDo is at the epicenter of Denver's urban renewal. The area has been completely transformed into a livable neighborhood with new, mid-rise condos, techy office buildings, high-end restaurants, and world-class microbreweries. It even has a new modern art museum, the Denver Museum of Contemporary Art. I hardly recognize it anymore, but that's probably a good thing. That's what's great about Denver: it's always reinventing itself.

Although LoDo is not an official Denver neighborhood, most locals regard it as the part of downtown northwest of Lawrence Street, southwest of Coors Field, east of Speer Boulevard, and south of the South Platte River.

Where It All Began: Larimer Square

Larimer St. between 14th and 15th St., Denver

Larimer Square is not actually a city square but a one-block stretch of Larimer Street in LoDo. It's the same block where William Larimer built his "square" of a log cabin foundation and founded Denver City in 1858 (yes, the street is named for him). The block soon became Denver's main commercial district in the 1860s and 1870s. In fact, most of the restored buildings on this street date to the late 19th century. Unfortunately, the whole block was almost demolished in the 1960s to make room for skyscrapers, but prominent preservationist Dana Crawford led an effort to save it from the wrecking ball.

It's a good thing, too, because Larimer Square gives downtown some Western charm and has since become one of the city's most popular destinations. It's lined with fantastic restaurants, unique independent shops, and bars with views of the Rocky Mountains. It seems like it's always busy in the evenings, and even more so on weekends. During the pandemic, the street was closed to traffic and filled with pop-up restaurants, art installations, and live music. If the street closure becomes permanent, as its operators hope, it will only make the Square more popular. Take some time to peruse the many interesting and unique shops on either side of the street, like the clothing stores Cotopaxi and Qinti.

Getting There: Walk north on the 16th Street Mall, turn left at Larimer Street and walk one block. The "Square" is between 14th and 15th Streets and may be closed to vehicular traffic.

Tip #8: About two-thirds of the way down the block on the left, stroll down the short alley into a beautiful, shaded courtyard; this is a cool place to explore more shops or to rest on a hot summer day.

Tip #9: Speaking of summer, if you're in Denver during a weekend in June, be sure to check out the Denver Chalk Art Festival in Larimer Square.

The street is closed and cleared for more than 200 chalk artists to create (temporary) works of art on the pavement. The festival also features live music. For more information, go to https://www.uncovercolorado.com/events/denver-chalk-art-festival.

All (Rail)Roads Lead to Union Station

1701 Wynkoop St., Denver

Union Station, at the north end of 17th Street, is close to the center of LoDo. After the original building opened in 1881, Union Station became the busiest building in Denver, serving railway passengers from all over the country. The structure helped give a young Denver the nickname "Queen City of the Plains," although "Mile High City" is much more popular today. However, the original depot quickly became outdated and was replaced in 1914 by the massive granite structure that still stands today.

By the 1970s, declining passenger train traffic almost spelled the end of Union Station. Except as a stop on Amtrak's *California Zephyr* and the terminus for the Winter Park Ski Train (now called the Winter Park Express), Union Station had become mostly deserted. However, the impressive structure got a new lease on life when it became the main hub of Denver's new light rail system in the 1990s. Today, 9 of Denver's 14 light and commuter rail lines converge on Union Station. In addition, thousands of new passengers passing through the area have led to the emergence of several upscale restaurants in the east and west wings of Union Station, including Tavernetta and Mercantile Dining & Provision.

When you enter Union Station through its main doorway, you'll marvel at the gilded, early 20th-century Great Hall with its 30-foot-high arched windows and grand chandeliers. Stop for a rest on the benches to take it all in. Union Station was renovated in 2014, and the lobby was redesigned to be more inviting, making it what some like to call "Denver's living room."

Getting There: After visiting Larimer Square, walk back toward the 16th Street Mall, proceed to 17th Street, and turn left. Union Station is four blocks down, and the main entrance will be directly in front of you on Wynkoop Street.

Tip #10: For an added sense of history, walk through the Great Hall toward the north side door and look for the tiled corridor. There, you'll find photos and artwork of Union Station's early days as Denver's main transport hub.

Tip #11: If you're flying out of Denver, free yourself from the hassle of driving in traffic by catching the new commuter ALine to Denver International Airport from Union Station. It's a direct, 37-minute ride and costs only $10.50, far less than a taxi or Uber ride to the airport.

The Microbrewery Revolution: Wynkoop Brewing Company

1634 18th St., Denver

Across the street from Union Station is the Wynkoop Brewing Company, a Denver institution not to be missed. Founded in 1988 in the century-old J.S. Brown Mercantile Building, Wynkoop Brewing was the first microbrewery, or brewpub, in Denver and one of the first of its kind in the country. Its pioneering founders included John Hickenlooper, who became Denver's mayor and Colorado's governor and is now one of Colorado's senators.

The popularity of Wynkoop Brewing, founded when LoDo was a sketchy and seldom-visited place, soon led to other new businesses in the area, especially other brewpubs. Today, metro Denver is home to more than 150 microbreweries, and it can be said that Wynkoop Brewing was the catalyst for the microbrewery revolution that has swept the country. It was also the catalyst for the transformation of LoDo from "skid row" into arguably Denver's most popular neighborhood.

By now, you're probably ready to wrap up your one-day tour of Denver with a tall cold one. You're in luck because Wynkoop Brewery has on tap dozens of the most interesting beers in the area, including the ones they brew on-site. So as you walk in, take a peek at their giant steel casks next to the long bar to appreciate where the revolution began.

Getting There: After exiting the main entrance of Union Station, turn left and walk half a block to the corner of Wynkoop and 18th Streets. The main entrance is on 18th Street.

Tip #12: Weather-permitting, snag a table on Wynkoop's elevated outdoor patio for great people-watching.

Be sure to try their flagship beer, the Rail Yard Ale. If beer is not your thing, they also have a big selection of wine and cocktails. And if you've never had bison before, try their scrumptious bison burger. You're out West, after all!

Chapter Review

Now you've covered many of Denver's most popular attractions in just a day and, hopefully, have gotten a good sense of Denver's unique Western flavor. You pulled it off by staying in Upper Downtown, which is central to all the places in this chapter, and you saved time by walking and taking the 16th Street Mall shuttle. But, first, let's recap what you've seen and done:

- You took a one-hour guided tour of Colorado's **State Capitol Building**. You saw its unique, gold-leaf dome and got a picture next to the step with the engraving "One Mile Above Sea Level." Inside, you gazed up at the dome from its marble-laden rotunda.

- You took a one-hour guided tour of the **Molly Brown House**, the mansion where Denver's most famous resident lived most of her life. You got an appreciation for Margaret Brown's early contribution to making Denver the vibrant city it is today.
- You rode the MallRide shuttle and strolled along the **16th Street Mall**, the 1.25-mile-long pedestrian corridor at the heart of downtown Denver. For lunch, you got a taste of the Old West at the saloon-style West of Surrender.
- You soaked in Denver's history at **Larimer Square** in LoDo and shopped in some of Denver's most unique stores.
- You walked to the newly restored **Union Station** in the heart of LoDo and took in the beautiful Great Hall.
- You experienced great brews and food at **Wynkoop Brewing Company**, which has become a Denver institution. It's where the transformation of LoDo and the microbrewery revolution in the U.S. began.

Chapter 2: How to Experience the Best of Denver in Two Days

Overview

Perhaps you've come to Denver for a convention and want to take an extra two days to get to know the city better. Or maybe you're on a cross-country road trip and want to spend more than a night in the Mile High City. Whatever your motivation, two full days in Denver will give you ample time to experience some of the best things to see and do here.

Our two-day tour starts by following Chapter 1 of this guide (starting on page XX). There, you'll get a good orientation to downtown and the main attractions close to it. For Day Two of the tour, we cover here in Chapter 2, we expand on what you've already seen downtown. Day Two will take you a little farther afield to the Golden Triangle, Denver's main arts district just south of downtown, and City Park, which is in East Denver. Because of that, you may wish to rent a car for the second day. If not, taxis and Ubers are easily available and will cost a lot less, and a bus ride to City Park will even cost less.

Tip #13: If you're not already staying downtown, consider staying in the Golden Triangle, where several new hotels have sprung up in recent years

The Golden Triangle is fairly central to all the places you'll visit on our two-day tour. The Element Denver Downtown East (1314 Elati St.) is a modern, budget-conscious option. For a more luxurious experience, try the beautiful new 4-star Art Hotel Denver (1201 N. Broadway).

See the Arts in the Golden Triangle

The triangle-shaped Golden Triangle neighborhood, bounded by Colfax Ave. on the north, Broadway on the east, and Speer Blvd. on the south, was long known, a bit plainly, as "Civic Center." In recent years, it's been more commonly referred to as the "Golden Triangle," probably because of the huge public investment in new arts facilities and museums that has drawn more visitors to the Mile High City. The fact that the Denver Mint is also here probably only lends to the area's "golden" reputation.

In 2016, the Golden Triangle was named the first Colorado Creative District for a good reason. It contains eight of Denver's finest museums, two of which are on our tour below. In 2017, Denver voters approved nearly $1 billion in bonds to improve and expand the neighborhood's institutions. If history is any guide, future visitors and tax revenues will more than make up for the investment. The New York Times has already called the neighborhood one of "the best places to visit" in the United States.

World-Renowned: Denver Art Museum

100 W. 14th Ave. Pkwy., Denver

The world-renowned Denver Art Museum (DAM) is at the heart of the Golden Triangle. It's been called the largest art museum between Chicago and Los Angeles. It also houses the world's largest collection of North American indigenous art. And it seems like every time I've visited in the last 30 years, the DAM has only expanded in size.

When the tall, brownish Martin Building opened in 1971, critics and residents alike were aghast at its non-traditional design. I have to admit that when I was younger, I didn't like its weird angles and small windows! After a four-year renovation, the Martin Building reopened in 2021 with a new addition, the glass-enclosed Sie Welcome Center.

The DAM went all-in on the weird angles when it opened the innovative Frederic C. Hamilton Building in 2006. Many regard this building as a work of art in itself, and I have to agree. Daniel Libeskind, the architect, says the geometric design is meant to evoke the angled peaks and geologic crystals of the nearby Rocky Mountains.

Getting There: Start your second day of our tour at the DAM's Hamilton Building when the museum opens at 10 am. (It's open daily from 10 am to 5 pm and 9 pm on Tuesdays; advance tickets are available online here: https://www.denverartmuseum.org/en/plan-your-visit.) Then, take an hour to peruse some of the museum's 12 collections spanning the globe. Optionally, if you're an art enthusiast, you may want to extend your time at the DAM and cut short your time at the much smaller Clyfford Still Museum, which is next.

Tip #14: After getting your ticket, start your self-guided tour of the DAM by riding the crisscrossing escalators to the top floor.

This way, you can fully appreciate the innovative angled design of the interior and maybe catch some mind-blowing art that makes interesting use of the space along the way.

Totally Unique: Clyfford Still Museum

1250 Bannock St., Denver

If you felt overwhelmed at the Denver Art Museum, the two-story Clyfford Still Museum will feel much more manageable. Even so, it's said to be the largest art museum in the world devoted to a single artist. He still was not from Denver, but he did live in Colorado for a good part of his life. This spacious museum was specifically designed to hold and display Still's work; the collection holds 93% of his output.

Clyfford Still is often considered one of the most important American painters of the 20th century and is certainly deserving of his own museum. Many of his Abstract Expressionist works are huge, colorful, and eye-popping. Even if you're not an art-lover, I bet you'll find his work impressive.

Getting There: The Clyfford Still Museum is conveniently located on the same block as the DAM's Hamilton Building. After exiting the Hamilton, turn left and proceed half a block down 13th Avenue. You'll see the Clyfford Still on the left. Allow a half-hour to an hour to see this collection. Tickets can be purchased in person or online here: https://clyffordstillmuseum.org/plan-your-visit/hours-and-tickets/.

Lunch at City, O' City

206 E. 13th Ave., Denver

City, O' City, which my vegetarian cousin introduced me to a few years ago, has become my favorite restaurant in the Golden Triangle. As an independent restaurant with a hipsterish vibe, you won't find anything else like it in Denver. Sure, it's a vegetarian restaurant, but even meat lovers will be hard-pressed not to find something they love here. The "chicken and waffles"—a waffle covered with bourbon-brined chicken-fried cauliflower—is mouth-watering good and my favorite dish on the menu.

Getting There: After exiting the Clyfford Still Museum, turn right on 13th Avenue and walk three blocks to City, O' City. Take about an hour to enjoy lunch and soak in the hipster Denver vibe.

Tip #15: As one of Denver's most popular restaurants, it's a good idea to make a reservation at City, O' City if you don't want to spend a long time waiting for a table. Lunchtime on weekdays can be especially busy. Reservations can be made by calling 303-831-6443.

Tip #16: Take a few minutes to browse the artwork on the walls. It's all produced by local artists and is for sale. City, O' City features different artists every month.

Explore the Attractions of City Park

Best Views in the City at City Park

Main entrance at E. 17th Ave. and City Park Esplanade, Denver

Established in 1882 on 330 acres, City Park is Denver's oldest and largest urban park. Mayor Robert Speer added a number of amenities to the park in the early 20th century as part of the City Beautiful Movement, and further enhancements were made in time for the Democratic National Convention in 2008. As a result, the park remains one of the best places in the city to capture a perfect photo of downtown skyscrapers framed by the Rocky Mountains.

Walking the Mile High Loop is a great way to see most of City Park in a short amount of time. The gravel-covered Mile High Loop was created in 2009 to take pedestrians by the park's main attractions. Start the loop at the park entrance at 17th Avenue and City Park Esplanade. To the left, you'll see the first of several markers marking an elevation of 5,280 feet (one mile) above sea level. The Colorado Memorial Fountain in front of you is also exactly one mile above sea level.

Follow the gravel-covered path to the left, going clockwise around the park. First, you'll pass the old Lowenstein Theatre and the Graham-Bible House, which used to house park superintendents. Then, at 22nd Avenue, you'll see the historic McClellan Gateway. Next, you'll come upon the Martin Luther King Memorial, the peach-colored Pavilion and Bandstand, the Burns Garden (named after poet Robert Burns), and the Sopris Garden. Soon, on the left, you'll see Duck Lake, which is part of the Denver Zoo. On the right is Ferril Lake, named after Thomas Ferril, a Colorado Poet Laureate.

As you're going by Ferril Lake, you'll come upon the park meadow and see the Denver Museum of Nature and Science on the other side. Depart the gravel trail here and proceed to the museum's west entrance for the next part of the tour.

Getting There: To start your tour of City Park, take a taxi, Uber, or Bus 20 on 17th Avenue to the 17th Avenue and Esplanade entrance of City Park. Plan to arrive by 1:30 pm; it's about a 12-minute ride by car from the Golden Triangle. Then, allow 60-90 minutes to walk the part of the Mile High Loop described in this section.

Tip #17: Before entering the Museum of Nature & Science, go up the west steps near the museum fountain and turn around to face west.

On a clear day, you'll get a fantastic view of downtown Denver in front of the Rocky Mountains and snow-capped Mt. Evans. This is the perfect place to capture a classic photo of Denver.

Tip #18: If you're in Denver during the summer, you're in luck! Be sure to check out the free jazz concerts every Sunday evening at the Pavilion in City Park.
Visit http://cityparkjazz.org for more information.

A National Treasure: Denver Museum of Nature & Science

2001 Colorado Blvd., Denver

When I was in high school, there was a huge buzz about the temporary Ramses II exhibit at the Denver Museum of Natural History (what the museum was called then). Everyone in town was talking about it, and it drew sell-out crowds. I was fortunate to see it, which helped foster my fascination with the wider world. As one of the few stops in the U.S. for the traveling exhibition, Ramses II also helped foster international acclaim for the Denver Museum of Natural History.

Today, the renamed Denver Museum of Nature & Science is by far the most visited natural history museum in the U.S. and the second-most visited museum overall. Even during the pandemic in 2020, the museum drew nearly 1 million visitors. The museum has one of the world's largest paleontology programs, and as such, the enormous dinosaur exhibits are truly amazing. In the main lobby, visitors are greeted by one of the largest and most complete Tyrannosaurus Rex skeletons on display anywhere.

Also, be sure not to miss the impressive Prehistoric Journey, Space Odyssey, Gems & Minerals, and Egyptian Mummies exhibits. Go to https://www.dmns.org/visit/ for ticket prices and the latest visitor information.

Getting There: Plan to begin your tour of the museum around 3 pm. This will give you two hours to take in the main exhibits before the museum closes at 5 pm. There is usually plenty of free parking in the lots adjacent to the museum.

Tip #19: In need of a rest? Watch a short film at the IMAX Theatre in Phipps Auditorium on the second floor (more info at: https://www.dmns.org/visit/imax/) or catch an astronomy show at the Gates Planetarium on the first floor.

The Flavor of the Old West: Buckhorn Exchange

1000 Osage St., Denver

I have met people on the East Coast who've told me that the Buckhorn Exchange steakhouse was their most memorable experience in Denver. So if you're looking for a unique, Western dining experience, this is one of the best places to get it.

Established in 1893, the Buckhorn Exchange is Denver's oldest continuously operated restaurant. Adding to the restaurant's Western cred, Henry H. "Shorty Scout" Zietz, the Buckhorn's founder, performed as a boy with Buffalo Bill Cody and his traveling Wild West show. Moreover, four sitting U.S. presidents have dined here, starting with Teddy Roosevelt in 1905.

When you enter the Buckhorn, you'll immediately notice it's not like other restaurants. Adorning the walls are close to 500 taxidermied animals, including deer, bison, a jackalope, and even a two-headed calf. The menu is equally exotic and includes Rocky Mountain oysters (calf testicles), rattlesnake, buffalo ribs, and elk steak. If you're not into Western delicacies, the Buckhorn has plenty of beef steak and salmon dishes.

Getting There: The Buckhorn is a little out of the way, so you'll probably want to take a taxi or Uber from your hotel in the Golden Triangle or downtown. If you are driving, you should be able to find plenty of free street parking.

Tip #20: Given the Buckhorn's enduring popularity, reservations around dinner time are a good idea. Just give them a call at 303-534-9505. You can also find their full menu at: https://www.buckhorn.com/menus.

Chapter Review

In this chapter, we covered the second day of your two-day tour of Denver. You expanded on what you saw downtown on Day One. On Day Two, you visited the center of Denver's thriving arts scene in the Golden Triangle; then, you ventured to City Park and its many attractions. Here's what you did in detail:

- You started the day at the eye-catching Hamilton Building of the **Denver Art Museum** and took in some of the museum's 12 collections from all over the world.
- Next, you went next door to the **Clyfford Still Museum**, the largest art museum in the world devoted to a single artist. Hopefully, you were impressed by his huge Abstract Expressionist artworks.
- You then walked a few blocks to the bustling **City, O' City** vegetarian restaurant, filled up on some tasty morsels, and got a feel for Denver's hipster scene.
- After lunch, you took motorized transportation to the 17th Avenue and Esplanade entrance of **City Park** and walked part of the Mile High Loop. Along the way, you saw some beautiful gardens, historic structures, several mile-high markers, and a great view of Denver.

- You toured the most visited natural history museum in the U.S., the impressive **Denver Museum of Nature & Science**. Among other exhibits, you saw huge dinosaurs, dazzling gems, and Egyptian mummies.
- For dinner, you got a memorable taste of the Old West at the **Buckhorn Exchange** steakhouse. If you were adventurous, you tried some Western delicacies like Rocky Mountain oysters and rattlesnake.as

Chapter 3: How to Experience the Best of Denver in Three Days

Overview

If you're in Denver for a long weekend, or you just want to extend your stay, you can cover a lot of ground and get a good sense of what makes Denver unique in three days. Start your three-day tour by following Chapters 1 and 2 in this guide. This chapter will cover Day Three of your tour of the Mile High City.

Day Three goes even farther afield than Days One and Two by taking you to the River North (RiNo) Art District just northeast of downtown and the Rocky Mountain foothills roughly 12 miles southwest of downtown. If you pick only one day to rent a car, Day Three would be the day to do it to help maximize your time. However, a taxi or Uber might still cost less depending on the prices of car rentals when you book.

Tip #21: If you're looking for a hotel for a three-day stay in Denver, I would look first in the LoDo area.

LoDo will be central to everything we cover in this guide's three-day tour. The Hotel Indigo (1801 Wewatta St.) is an attractive boutique hotel that is less expensive than other options in the area. However, if you want a truly luxurious experience, consider the beautiful 4-star Crawford Hotel (1701 Wynkoop St.) directly above Union Station.

Experience the RiNo Art District

The River North (RiNo) Art District is one of the latest examples of Denver reinventing itself. RiNo, which encompasses parts of the Five Points, Globeville, and Elyria-Swansea neighborhoods immediately northeast of downtown, was long the industrial hub of Denver. When industry began to move out of Denver in the 1980s and 1990s, many empty warehouses and abandoned buildings were left behind in this area. The suddenly cheap rents attracted artists and craftspeople, and the area soon became an artist colony.

In 2005, local artists established the RiNo Art District to promote the area's many creative businesses, including architects, art galleries, painters, furniture makers, and photographers. As is almost inevitable with successful art districts, gentrification has followed, and new mid-rise condos, high-end restaurants, and music venues have also arrived. But they haven't detracted from the artsy-industrial vibe you'll get in the Larimer Street corridor between North Broadway and North Downing Streets. If anything, the slew of new businesses has made RiNo one of Denver's buzziest and most interesting parts.

Tips #22: If you're in Denver on a Friday evening in late spring or summer, check out the Friday Night Bazaar between 4 pm and 9 pm. Between 24th and 25th Streets, Larimer Street turns into a night market full of craft and fashion vendors, beer stalls, food trucks, and live music.

It's a fun way to experience RiNo, it's family- and dog-friendly, and entry is free! Go to https://rinoartdistrict.org/do/friday-night-bazaar-2021 for the latest information.

Art on Display: Mural Walking Tour

Larimer St. between 24th St. and 27th St., Denver

One of my favorite features of RiNo is the ever-changing display of murals on the sides of many buildings. The eye-popping colors and unusual designs created by local artists let you know that you're in a thriving arts district. They're not hard to find in RiNo: More than 100 dot the neighborhood, including 50 documented by the district in one eight-square-block area alone. Street murals are becoming popular in urban areas throughout the country, but you would be hard-pressed to find a greater concentration than in the RiNo District.

Start your one-hour walking tour around 10 am at the corner of North Broadway and Arapahoe Street. There, you won't be able to miss the giant "Denver: Love This City" mural. This is a famous selfie spot and <u>the</u> place to get your Denver selfie. Next, walk two blocks north on Broadway, turn right onto Larimer Street, and walk two more blocks to 24th Street. On this block, you'll start to notice more murals.

Check out the giant hummingbird mural near the corner of 24th and Larimer Streets. Then walk half a block north and turn right into the RiNo Art Alley, where murals of all shapes and sizes adorn the walls. One of my favorites is the zebra-like black-and-white mural by A.L. Grime. Next, continue one block to 27th Street and turn right to get back on Larimer Street. There, you can't miss the huge "Larimer Boy/Girl" mural that dominates the block; from one end, the mural shows a boy, but by the time you get to the other end, the perspective has changed, and the same mural shows a girl.

Getting There: Drive or take an Uber to the triangular corner of North Broadway, Arapahoe Street, and Park Avenue. If driving, you should be able to find plenty of free or metered street parking.

Tip #23: Every month, the RiNo Art District sponsors the RiNo Mural Program, which brings in artists from around the world to create new murals in recognition of events like Black History Month, Womxn's History Month, and Gay Pride. Check out their schedule at <u>https://rinoartdistrict.org/visit/events-calendar</u>, and you just might be able to watch artists creating their mural masterpieces.

<u>Shop at Modern Nomad</u>

2936 Larimer St., Denver

Modern Nomad is a one-of-a-kind design and home décor collective in the heart of RiNo. It houses about ten retailers in a remodeled cavernous 5,500-square-foot warehouse. Modern Nomad is one of the best representations of RiNo's artsy vibe. It's also the perfect place to pick up unique items for the home or get ideas on how to completely redecorate. Their website describes the space as a "three-dimensional living magazine."

Plan to arrive after 11 am when Modern Nomad opens. Once inside, check out Modern Home Design for decorating ideas, Atla Design for hand-crafted furnishings, or CBCXOXO for sterling silver, copper, and costume jewelry.

Getting There: After finishing the mural walking tour, turn back onto Larimer Street and continue walking northeast for two and a half blocks. Modern Nomad is on the right and unmissable; just look for the big "Empire" sign.

Tip #24: Modern Nomad periodically offers on-site workshops and pop-ups for anyone interested in home decorating. Sign up for their mailing list at https://www.modernnomaddenver.com/events to be informed of upcoming events.

Lunch at Denver Central Market

2669 Larimer St., Denver

Denver Central Market is like the big urban food markets of old and is similar in concept to Modern Nomad. The market brings about a dozen food vendors under one roof offering everything from fresh meats and artisanal bread to homemade ice cream. There are a variety of mouth-watering eateries, too, making this an excellent place to stop for lunch. For high-quality seafood, try Tammen's Fish Market. Green Seed offers smoothies and salads made from locally grown produce. And the wood-fired pizza and handmade pasta at Vero Italian will satisfy the biggest appetites.

Getting There: After exiting Modern Nomad, turn left and walk about three blocks to Denver Central Market; it will be on your right. (Don't forget to look for more murals along the way!) Plan to arrive by noon and take about 45 minutes for lunch.

Tip #25: When ready to sit down and enjoy lunch, look for the brightly painted artist tables in the main food hall. Each table was designed and painted by a Denver artist, and they certainly add credence to RiNo's slogan "Where Art Is Made."

Explore the Rocky Mountain Foothills

About eight miles west of downtown Denver, the Front Range of the Rocky Mountains begins to rise from the flatlands of the High Plains. The change from plains to mountains is abrupt, and almost any vehicle (or pair of legs) will feel the strain of starting the climb. The elevation increases 1,200 feet in just the first 10 miles of the climb on I-70 going west. Locals refer to this first set of hills, mesas, and low mountains as "the foothills," with peaks as high as 10,000 feet above sea level. Here the air is noticeably cooler, the ground (sometimes) greener, and the endless views of the flatlands more extensive. Welcome to the Rockies!

Marking the beginning of the Rockies proper is the Dakota Hogback, a long narrow ridge that seems to point about 60° toward the higher peaks. It points this way because it is the easternmost edge of the ground that lifted up when the Rocky Mountains started forming about 80 million years ago. The Hogback stretches from Wyoming to New Mexico and forms the core of some unusual rock formations, including those of Red Rocks Amphitheatre, which we visit below.

Sitting at the foot of the Hogback is the small town of Morrison, a charming, old-fashioned settlement that is the gateway to Red Rocks and the other attractions we'll explore on this afternoon of Day Three.

Perfect Sound at Red Rocks Park & Amphitheatre

18300 W. Alameda Pkwy., Morrison

Red Rocks Amphitheatre may well be the most famous and most celebrated concert venue in the world. And for a good reason. Carved out of red sandstone rock formations overlooking Denver and possessing near-perfect natural acoustics, Red Rocks makes any performance memorable. When I was a teenager and young adult, Red Rocks was the place to see the likes of Michael Jackson and U2. In fact, many rock bands have recorded live concerts here and sold them as special albums.

Red Rocks impressed the earliest White settlers in the region, and it wasn't long until it became a local tourist attraction. As early as 1911, famous opera singer Mary Garden sang "Ave Maria" here and later wrote: "Never in any opera house, the world over, have I found more perfect acoustic properties" than those at Red Rocks. Others agreed, and in 1941, the Civilian Conservation Corps finished building the 10,000-seat outdoor amphitheater that is still in use today. The Beatles' 1964 concert propelled Red Rocks to international fame. In 2003, the venue underwent a major renovation, including constructing a modern visitor center.

Today, the park hosts not only rock concerts but all kinds of musical performances, educational events, film screenings, and even high school graduations. For the full schedule of events, visit the park's calendar at: https://www.redrocksonline.com/events/?view=calendar.

Take about 45 minutes to peruse the exhibits in the visitor center, including the Red Rocks Performers Hall of Fame and the Colorado Music Hall of Fame. If time allows, watch the short film by Oscar-winning director Donna Dewey about memorable concerts at Red Rocks. Be sure to allow at least 20 minutes for a self-guided tour of the amphitheater itself.

Getting There: The easiest way to get to Red Rocks is to drive there (or hire a car). From downtown, take I-25 north and exit onto westbound I-70. Go about 15 miles, then take exit 259 onto southbound County Highway 93/Hogback Road. Then, go about 1 mile, turn right onto West Alameda Parkway and follow the signs to the parking lots. Plan to arrive by 1:15 pm. Parking and admission to the visitor center are free.

Note: It's important to arrive before 2:00 pm, when the park often closes, in preparation for night events. Call 720-865-2494 to learn if and when the park is closing early on the day of your visit. If there are no events, the park is open to the public until one hour after sunset.

Tip #26: Go to the top of the benches just below Creation Rock in the amphitheater and exercise your vocal cords. You'll be amazed at just how good the acoustics of Red Rocks really are!

Dig for Fossils at Dinosaur Ridge

16831 W. Alameda Pkwy., Morrison

If you didn't get enough of dinosaurs at the Denver Museum of Nature & Science, Dinosaur Ridge is the place to get more. It's said to be one of the top dinosaur track sites in the country. A Colorado School of Mines geology professor first discovered fossilized dinosaur bones here in 1877. However, the construction of West Alameda Parkway through the hogback in the 1930s revealed significantly more fossils. In fact, this is where the first Stegosaurus skeleton in the world was found. Acknowledging its importance to paleontology, the National Park Service designated the area a National Natural Landmark in 1973.

Dinosaur Ridge is also a great place to learn about the geology of Colorado and how the Rocky Mountains were formed. Geologists offer two-hour guided walking tours along the Dinosaur Ridge and Triceratops Trails; visit https://dinoridge.org/visit-dinosaur-ridge/public-tours/ to book a tour.

Outside the visitor center, you'll notice full-size dinosaur replicas; this is a good spot to get some photos. The visitor center has many interactive displays, including simulated dig sites that kids will love; little ones can even take home souvenir fossils. On good weather days, take 1-2 hours to hike either the Dinosaur Ridge Trail or the Triceratops Trail; both are paved. Keep your eyes peeled for the more than 300 dinosaur tracks found near them.

Getting There: Even though you can walk to Dinosaur Ridge from Red Rocks, driving there will save you some time. After exiting the parking lots at Red Rocks, turn right onto County Highway 93/Hogback Road and go about a mile to the town of Morrison. Bear left onto Highway 8/Bear Creek Avenue, then immediately join C-470 northbound. Take the first exit for West Alameda Parkway and follow the signs to the Dinosaur Ridge Visitor Center. Plan to arrive by 2:15 pm; the park closes at 4 pm.

Tip #27: Take one of the 45-minute guided shuttle tours that follow the main trails to get the most out of a short visit. At several stops, an expert guide will interpret the dinosaur tracks and bone fossils found along the way. Call 303-697-3466 to make advanced reservations, which are recommended.

Unique Colorado Experience at The Fort

19192 Colorado Hwy. 8, Morrison

When I first dined at The Fort restaurant in college, I was amazed at the variety of dishes. I didn't know Colorado cuisine could be so exotic! Some describe The Fort as a high-end steakhouse, but I say it's much more than that. Historian Sam Arnold built The Fort in 1963 as a full-size replica of Bent's Old Fort, a historic trading post on the Santa Fe Trail in southeastern Colorado. The cuisine, best described as a fusion of Native American, Mexican, and modern American, is meant to evoke the frontier food of the early 19th century. Whatever you call it, the food at The Fort is outstanding and often called the best in the state.

Some of my favorite cocktails are found here. Try the prickly-pear margarita or their signature Hailstorm Julep. The variety of buffalo (bison) is astounding and tasty, from filet mignon and ribeye to BBQ ribs. More exotic fare includes Rocky Mountain oysters (deep-fried calf testicles in panko and a sweet chili sauce), wild boar sausage, pickled quail eggs wrapped in bison sausage, braised bison tongue, elk medallions, and grilled quail. Add their excellent service and remarkable views of Denver; you won't soon forget your dining experience at The Fort.

Getting There: From Dinosaur Ridge, get back on C-470 going southbound. Take the second exit at U.S. Highway 285 and go west about one and a half miles. Take the first exit north onto Colorado Highway 8; The Fort will be about 1000 feet ahead on the right. The restaurant opens by 5:30 pm every night except Monday when it's closed. Reservations are essential. You can book on OpenTable or by calling 303-697-4771.

Tip #28: Get an extra helping of history with your meal by booking one of The Fort's monthly dinner lectures sponsored by the Tesoro Cultural Center.

Experts on the history of the Southwest speak on a variety of related topics while you savor a pre-set menu. Visit https://www.tesoroculturalcenter.org/historic-lecture-series/ to learn more and to book your dinner lecture.

Chapter Review

In this chapter, you wrapped up your three-day tour of Denver and discovered the best of what Denver has to offer. On Day Three, you experienced the RiNo Art District and some attractions near Morrison in the Rocky Mountain foothills, which helped bring to life the unique Western character of Denver. In detail, here is what you did:

- You took a self-guided **Mural Walking Tour** in the RiNo Art District. You saw some of the most colorful and eye-popping designs you'll see in any urban landscape.
- You shopped at the home design collective **Modern Nomad**, which has about ten vendors that can help you add a little hipster flair to your home or help you completely redecorate.
- You had a delicious lunch at **Denver Central Market** and enjoyed the artist-painted tables. Hopefully, you topped it off with some artisanal ice cream or delectable chocolates.

- You ventured west into the Rocky Mountain foothills and experienced the grandeur of **Red Rocks Amphitheatre**, with its perfect acoustics and its place in music history.
- You took pictures with dinosaurs, dug for fossils, and learned about the geology of the Rocky Mountains at **Dinosaur Ridge**, a National Natural Landmark.
- You dined at the incomparable restaurant at **The Fort**, a full-size replica of historic Bent's Old Fort. Hopefully, you sampled some Colorado delicacies like Rocky Mountain oysters or grilled quail.

Chapter 4: Experience Denver Like a Local – Downtown

Overview

If you started reading this guide from the beginning, you already know we've covered a lot of things to see and do in Denver. From the gold-covered State Capitol and historic LoDo neighborhood to some of the impressive art museums of the Golden Triangle and the higher terrain of the Rocky Mountain Foothills, we hit many of the major hotspots that tourists seek out and that make Denver memorable.

But if you really want to get to know Denver, there's so much more to see and experience. Perhaps you're in Denver for your second, third, or fourth visit, and you're looking for something new to do. Or maybe you've recently moved to Denver (like so many others) and want to get to know Denver like a local. In either case, the rest of this guide will help you look and sound like a Denverite in no time.

In this chapter, we'll focus on the many other well-known and less well-known attractions of Downtown Denver. We'll cover fun things to do, interesting places to visit, and delectable places to dine. We'll cover Lower and Upper Downtown plus the adjacent neighborhoods that most locals consider part of the greater downtown area: the Golden Triangle, Auraria, RiNo, and Capitol Hill.

Tip #29: Denver locals may differ slightly on what they consider "downtown," but I think most would agree that downtown proper includes the central business district bounded by I-25 on the north and west, Colfax Avenue on the south, and Lincoln Street/North Broadway on the east. Another way to know you're in downtown proper is when you're on the streets that run diagonally to the north-south and east-west grid.

LoDo (Lower Downtown)

As we mentioned in Chapter 1, LoDo is where Denver began in the late 1850s, and in the 21st century, it has become the epicenter of Denver's urban renewal. In the first chapter, we described some things that make LoDo special, like the enduring historical charm of Larimer Square; the hub of Denver's rail network, Union Station; and the spark of the microbrewery revolution Wynkoop Brewing Company. These places are not just enjoyed by tourists but are essential parts of the Denver landscape that every local should know.

Of course, there's much more to LoDo—so much, in fact, that it would be nearly impossible to experience everything in a weekend, much less a day. So instead, I would advise taking several weekends to explore LoDo. No matter how you go about it, you're bound to have fun and learn much more about Denver in the process.

Brunch at The Delectable Egg

1642 Market St., Denver, and other locations

One of my favorite memories of going to college and working downtown was having a breakfast-style lunch at The Delectable Egg with my mom. I would usually get a skillet with house potatoes, scrambled eggs, and veggies, which would always leave me full.

The Delectable Egg is still a great, affordably priced place to fill up for a day of activities in LoDo. Their success has allowed them to expand to several locations in Denver. They are well known for their many styles of scrumptious eggs Benedicts (they call them "Bennys"), including the Cowboy Benedict. Their Western-style omelets are also delicious and include, of course, the world-famous Denver omelet.

Daniels & Fisher Tower

1601 Arapahoe St., Denver

The Daniels & Fisher Tower is an iconic Denver landmark near the center of the 16th Street Mall. It also marks, in mind at least, where LoDo begins—so points northwest of here are in LoDo. The 372-foot tower was completed in 1911 as part of the Daniels & Fisher Department Store, the finest in the city at the time. When it was finished, the D&F Tower was said to be the third-tallest structure in the world and the tallest west of the Mississippi River. It was designed to resemble Saint Mark's Campanile in Venice, Italy.

Daniels & Fisher was bought out by May Department Stores in the 1950s and in Denver became May D&F, which I always associated with the tower in my youth. The D&F Tower, as locals call it, nearly succumbed to the urban renewal demolitions that took place in the 1960s and 1970s, but fortunately, it was spared. Unfortunately, the adjoining department store was not so lucky, so the tower stands alone today. When Macy's bought out May Department Stores in 2005, the D&F name disappeared from Denver except for the D&F Tower.

Today, the D&F Tower's small floors are occupied by offices, and its lobby is usually inaccessible to the public. However, you can still get a great selfie with Denver's iconic landmark about one block northwest or southeast of the tower. Come see the tower after sunset when it comes to life with Night Lights Denver, a rotation of digital art that is projected onto the tower's face. The lights at Christmas are especially beautiful, and, if you can brave the cold, the tower is usually the focus of a New Year's Eve fireworks display.

Tip #30: You can get a peek inside the tower if you visit Lannie's Clocktower Cabaret, which performs weekend shows in the vintage cabaret space below the tower.

There's a variety of music, burlesque, comedy, drag, and circus performances, sometimes all in one night! The show I went to reminded me of a miniature Cirque du Soleil. It definitely makes for a fun night out. Visit their website at https://www.clocktowercabaret.com/for showtimes and tickets.

Tip #31: Each fall, the Denver Architecture Foundation hosts "Doors Open Denver," a week-long event that usually opens closed architectural spaces to the public.

One of them is often the 20th-floor observation deck of the D&F Tower. Guided tours are limited to small groups on weekends, so reservations are essential. Visit https://denverarchitecture.org/events-programs/doorsopendenver/ for more information.

Skyline Park

Between 15th St. and 18th St. on Arapahoe St., Denver

Immediately adjacent to the D&F Tower on both sides is the "subtle" Skyline Park. It's a mostly paved linear public space that runs along Arapahoe Street between 15th and 18th Streets. The city calls it "a gathering place for the downtown community," and there usually is something fun going on. It was built in the 1970s with a somewhat bleak Modernist design, but the park has been upgraded several times since then. However, the original geometric fountains are still a pleasure on a hot day.

One of the park's main attractions is the ice-skating rink. In 2017, voters approved money to improve the park, including a permanent ice rink infrastructure. In the summer, between mid-June and late September, the park is the scene of the blocks-long Skyline Park Beer Garden. The beer garden celebrates Denver's ever-growing craft beer movement. It features 12 craft beers on tap, food vendors, Oktoberfest communal tables, live music on the weekends, and a game area with ping pong, miniature golf, and cornhole. It's open daily from 11 am to 10 pm, weather permitting. Go to https://www.skylinebeergarden.com/ for more information.

Tip #32: For a different taste of the West, look for Biker Jim's Gourmet Hot Dogs, which include Alaskan reindeer and elk meat hot dogs and buffalo sausages. Mmmm, my mouth is watering just thinking about it!

Tabor Center

1200 17th St., Denver

I can remember when the modern, glass-enclosed Tabor Shopping Center opened in 1984 on the 16th Street Mall. The Tabor Center's giant, three-story atrium; its upscale stores; and the new, modern 30-story skyscraper on top of it all seemed like a breath of fresh air in this once-decrepit part of LoDo. I'm sure that's what the Denver Urban Renewal Authority intended when it bulldozed most of the area for redevelopment in the 1970s. An unfortunate victim of their plan was the demolished five-story Tabor Block built on the current Tabor Center site in the late 19th century; it was long considered one of Denver's premier business addresses.

Unfortunately, the Tabor Center's modernity and a beautiful atrium were not a lasting draw for shoppers or diners. With its high-end stores, the shopping center struggled to survive the oil bust of the 1980s. I once visited during college only to find most of the indoor stores permanently closed.

Today, the revitalization of Lodo has changed the Tabor Center's fortunes. At the intersection of the 16th Street Mall, LoDo, and the 17th Street business district, the Tabor Center is once again a top business address in Denver. The complex houses Colorado Athletic Club's flagship fitness center, a WeWork office, numerous restaurants facing the Mall, and an adjoining Westin hotel. Although the atrium shops are no longer there, it's still worth a stroll inside the atrium, especially on a sunny day.

Tip #33: Looking to refuel? The Tabor Center features several good restaurants, including a Cheesecake Factory and the southwestern-style Blue Agave Grill. My favorite is the Mellow Mushroom, which makes fantastic pizzas.

Writer Square

1512 Larimer St., Denver

Writer Square, lined with red-hued bricks, is a charming block of shops, galleries, offices, and condos between the 16th Street Mall and Larimer Square. In fact, developer Geoie Writer designed the square to be a transition between the modern high rises of central downtown and the historic structures of Larimer Square. Completed in 1982, Writer Square was the first modern mixed-use development in Denver. Since then, it has won several design awards for its uniqueness.

In 2009, tenants decried a remodel meant "to bring the square into the 21st century." The remodel was intended to open up the central space to make it more appealing to shoppers. Despite the changes, I still think Writer Square gives this block of LoDo a more human scale and a nice European aesthetic. The shops seem to change frequently, but the Rocky Mountain Chocolate Factory (500 16th St. Mall) has been there for as long as I can remember; it must be one of the company's earliest stores (founded in Durango, Colorado, in 1981). If you're a chocolate lover, you'll be in heaven here, with its 300 different kinds of chocolatey confections. Be sure to try their signature "bear claw"—a claw-sized delight of caramel and nuts covered in chocolate.

Tip #34: Come to Writer Square at Christmas time; the bright white lights, large Christmas tree, and other festive decorations will soon put you in the holiday spirit. Look for pop-up Christmas stores that are ideal for picking up ornaments, other decorations, and gifts.

Comedy Works Downtown

1226 15th St., Denver

One of my favorite things to do after a busy week of work and attending college classes was to unwind at Comedy Works, Denver's first full-time professional comedy club (it opened in 1981). Located in a below-ground space in Larimer Square, just two blocks from where I went to school, it was easy to pop in for a stand-up comedy act or two. Back then, the tickets were really cheap or even free when audiences were thin. But because it's such an intimate space with low ceilings and chairs close to the stage, I couldn't help being infected with the reverberating laughter.

Today, Comedy Works is still Denver's premier location for stand-up comedy and one of the top spots in the country. It's where Roseanne Barr started with stand-up, and comic luminaries such as Jerry Seinfeld, Ellen DeGeneres, Chris Rock, and George Lopez have all performed here. More recently, Comedy Works has become known as the favorite recording place for Denver resident Josh Blue, the winner of the reality TV show "Last Comic Standing."

Tip #35: Because of the tremendous popularity of Comedy Works Downtown, it's a little more difficult to get tickets than when I went to college in the early 1990s.

Fortunately, Comedy Works has opened a second location in the southern suburb of Greenwood Village (Comedy Works South), which gives comedy-lovers more options. Visit the Comedy Works website at https://www.comedyworks.com/events for their latest shows and to buy tickets.

Bistro Vendome in Larimer Square

1420 Larimer St., Denver

The first time I dined at Bistro Vendome just off Larimer Square on a warm summer evening, I was blown away by the experience. Dining on the garden patio inside a small, brick-lined courtyard instantly transported me back to a small square in Paris. Not only was the food of exceptional quality, but the service was friendly and attentive without being overbearing (don't picture rude or indifferent French waiters!). I was impressed when the restaurant manager came to my table to ensure everything was okay and to engage me in conversation.

Bistro Vendome's style is classic French bistro cuisine, which is to say that it's hearty comfort food that will satisfy almost any appetite (don't picture minuscule portions!). Classic dishes include steak fries, duck confit, and French onion soup, but don't be afraid to try the escargot or mussels. And with 65 varieties of French wine, you're bound to find the perfect accompaniment for your meal. Of course, the hardest part is leaving room for dessert, but if you can manage it, the chocolate souffle is worth it!

Tip #36: To get an even fuller French experience, visit Bistro Vendome on select Monday evenings for the screening of a French film that goes with a five-course, prix-fixe menu.

Go to https://www.exploretock.com/bistrovendome to see their schedule of films. On other nights with comfortable weather, make a reservation for the beautiful and charming garden patio; because of its popularity, you may need to do this a week in advance. You can book on OpenTable by visiting the restaurant's website at https://bistrovendome.com/#reservations or by calling 303-825-3232.

Museum of Contemporary Art

1485 Delgany St., Denver

The Denver Museum of Contemporary Art (MCA) is the newest major art museum in Denver and one of its most interesting. The MCA moved into a beautiful and modern 27,000-square-foot facility in 2007, and since then, it has become an anchor for Denver's burgeoning LoDo district. MCA Denver says its vision is to welcome all audiences, celebrate all voices, and share all stories. It also seeks "to spark curiosity and conversation through world-class exhibitions and quirky programming." They also aim to be "both sophisticated and unpretentious"—which you could say also describes Denver in general.

When I visited MCA Denver in the summer of 2020, I could tell it was a museum aiming to be inclusive and a reflection of the modern world. The visiting exhibition at the time was called "Nari Ward— We the People," a celebration of a Jamaican-born contemporary artist who lives in Harlem, New York. The art was very approachable—no lines of tape and security alarms separated the visitor from the exhibits, which were all unusual and thought-provoking. The MCA is a must-see if you're an art fan in Denver. Visit their website at https://mcadenver.org/visit for the latest visitor information.

Tip #37: After perusing the museum's exhibits, take a break and visit the "green" rooftop café and bar.

Check out the native vegetation there, which helps soak up carbon dioxide and reduce the heat the roof emits. The bar has interesting cocktails and even a happy hour Tuesday through Thursday from 4 pm to 6 pm. You can take in some great views of LoDo and the 16th Street Mall while you sip your drink and munch on your snacks.

Millennium Bridge

North end of 16th St. Mall

The Millennium Bridge is a 200-foot pedestrian bridge made of suspended tubular steel. Completed in 2002, it was the first cable-stayed pedestrian bridge in the world. Close to the South Platte River, its main pillar was intended to resemble the giant mast of a ship, a lofty aspiration considering that the river is not deep enough for even large boats. In fact, only one ship has been reputed to reach Denver from Nebraska—a 19th-century, flat-bottomed steamboat that had to be dislodged from the river bottom many times during its journey.

The Millennium Bridge is still a remarkable sight to see, and it affords incredible views of the downtown skyline and the Rocky Mountains to the northwest. It crosses over train and light rail tracks while connecting the end of the 16th Street Mall at Chestnut Place to Commons Park on the South Platte River.

Tip #38: Even though the walking level of the bridge doesn't rise more than 25 feet, you don't have to do any climbing to appreciate the views from the bridge.

Glass-enclosed elevators at both ends of the bridge make traversing it a little easier. Visiting the bridge at night (it's open 24 hours) is even more impressive; the nighttime skyline is on brilliant display, and the giant mast itself is lit up with multiple, changing colors.

Riverfront Park

Northwest of Little Raven St. along South Platte River, Denver

The Riverfront Park area, where Cherry Creek flows into the South Platte River, was the home of some of Denver's earliest settlers. The narrow river floodplain was an encampment site for Arapahoe and Southern Cheyenne Native Americans, but when White men discovered gold in the South Platte, a flood of new settlers arrived. They quickly turned the area into a jumble of shacks, teepees, and log cabins. As Denver grew (even after the river gold quickly ran out), the floodplain became crowded with shanties often swept away by floods. By the 1970s, the riverfront had become an unsightly dumping ground until it was cleaned up and transformed into one of Denver's most beautiful urban parks.

"Riverfront Park" is not an official Denver Park, but it's what locals often call the several adjoining parks that line the South Platte River in LoDo. Riverfront Park comprises Fishback Park on the north side of the river, and on the south side, Centennial Gardens,

Confluence Park, Commons Park, and the City of Cuernavaca Park. Each is covered by green lawns and crossed by multiple gravel footpaths and paved bike paths. This area is most popular in summer and can draw thousands of people looking to cool off in the river on a hot day.

The beautiful Centennial Gardens are on the southwest side of Riverfront Park (southwest of Cherry Creek). Modeled on formal French gardens, the gardens display the typical neat hedgerows and fountains and many native, drought-tolerant plants and flowers. Where Elitch Circle turns into Little Raven Street under Speer Boulevard, be sure to check out the giant mural *Confluent People*, which depicts the diversity of Denver's people.

The appropriately named Confluence Park is where Cherry Creek empties into the South Platte. See the entry below for information on the bike trails that emanate from here and the kayaking options in summer.

To the northeast of Confluence Park is Commons Park. Its wide lawns make it a popular picnic spot on good-weather days, and its many jogging paths are popular with joggers year-round. On the north end of the park is the Downtown Denver Skatepark, one of the largest parks in the city, created especially for skateboarders.

The City of Cuernavaca Park is northeast of Commons Park and past the 20th Street viaduct. The park is named for Denver's sister city in Mexico, which also happens to be one mile above sea level. The park is equipped with bike trails, picnic areas, a baseball diamond, several soccer fields, and a parking area on its north end.

Tip #39: The Greenway Foundation, which aims to improve and build local stewardship for urban waterways, hosts multiple events in and near Riverfront Park each summer

Events include volunteer river clean-up days, art exhibits, and neighborhood festivals. Check out their website at https://www.thegreenwayfoundation.org/events.html to learn more.

Tip #40: Want to see more of the South Platte River? Take a ride on the historic streetcar that travels along the banks of the South Platte from Confluence Park south to Empower Field at Mile High (home of the Denver Broncos).

The Denver Trolley, usually operating in the summer only, makes a fun diversion for kids. Visit their website for more information: http://www.denvertrolley.org/.

Biking & Kayaking at Confluence Park

2250 15th St., Denver

Confluence Park is not only where Cherry Creek and the South Platte meet; it marks the confluence of two of Denver's great bike trails—the Cherry Creek Trail starts here and follows the creek 40 miles south to the town of Franktown. The trail is set 15 feet below street level, so it's easy to forget you're riding through a major urban area. Likewise, the South Platte River Trail runs through Confluence Park, extending 36 miles from Chatfield Reservoir in the south to the town of Brighton in the north. Both trails make for great day-long bike rides on one of Denver's many sunny days.

Confluence Park also has short kayaking and tubing runs on the South Platte—where else can you go kayaking in a downtown area? For the liveliest rapids, plan to kayak in May or June when the runoff from the mountains' melting snow is at its highest. But beware, the water will be cold, and you may want to bring a wetsuit to keep from freezing. The water in July and August is usually calmer and not quite as cold.

Tip #41: If you're new to kayaking or don't have your own equipment, fret not.

The nearby Confluence Kayak & Ski (2301 7th St., on the north side of the river) offers kayak, river tube, bike rentals, and kayaking lessons. Visit the website at https://www.denver.org/listing/confluence-kayaks/5041/ to book lessons or call 303-433-3676 for more information.

LoDo Microbrewery Tour

1001 16th St. or 1634 18th St., Denver

If you like beer, even just a little bit, then a tour of LoDo's famous microbreweries is surely on tap when you're in Denver. There's a reason Denver is called the "Napa Valley of Beer." Since the microbrewery revolution started here in the late 1980s at Wynkoop Brewing Company, the number of microbreweries has exploded to the point that Denver produces more than 200 varieties of craft beer every day.

One of the best ways to experience LoDo's microbreweries is to take the LoDo Craft Beer Tour hosted by Denver Microbrew Tours. It's a two-and-a-half-hour guided walking tour of the neighborhood's best-loved microbreweries. Along the 1.5-mile walk, you'll sample at least ten beers at four different breweries, learn how craft beer is made, and learn about some "scandalous Denver history tidbits." One of the stops is the original Rock Bottom brewery, which since opening in 1991, has expanded to locations all over the world.

The LoDo Craft Beer Tour is conducted on Fridays, Saturdays, and Sundays and departs from either Wynkoop Brewing or Rock Bottom in LoDo. Private tours can also be arranged. Visit Denver Microbrew Tours at https://www.denvermicrobrewtour.com/lodo-craft-beer-tour/ or call 303-578-9548 to book your tour. You can also find out about other beer tours at https://www.denver.org/denver-beer-week/denver-beer/brewery-tours/.

Tip #42: If you're a beer enthusiast, come to Denver in the fall for Denver Beer Week, when festivals, tap tastings, and other beer events take over the city—just in time for Oktoberfest.

Check out the city's website at https://www.denver.org/denver-beer-week/ for more information as fall approaches.

Tavernetta Restaurant

1889 16th St., Denver

Tavernetta, situated in a new stone-clad building behind Union Station, is probably my favorite restaurant in Denver. The atmosphere is casual and lively, and the open-kitchen layout adds even more authenticity. Best of all, the dolce vita–style Italian cuisine is out of this world. Established only in 2017 by James Beard Foundation winners Bobby Stuckey and chef Lachlan MacKinnon-Patterson, Tavernetta's chef Cody Cheetham has already garnered a James Beard nomination for best chef. And for a good reason. The pasta is made in-house, and the langoustines and other seafood are incredibly fresh. (When I was growing up in Denver, fresh seafood was hard to come by—but no more.) Most of all, the flavors are tantalizing to the tongue and paired with fantastic wine by an expert sommelier.

The dinner prices are not cheap, so you may be tempted to come only for a special occasion. Instead, consider Tavernetta's daily happy hour from 4 pm to 6 pm, offering interesting cocktails and appetizers for under $10. You can check out the full menu and make reservations at https://www.tavernettadenver.com/menus/.

Tip #43: If you want to experience Tavernetta's extensive wine menu without the big meal, visit Tavernetta's sister restaurant and wine bar, Sunday Vinyl, next door in Union Station (1803 16th St.).

The small plates, wines by the glass, and vinyl-spun music make for a perfect Sunday brunch or light dinner during the week. See the full menu at https://www.sundayvinyl.com/menus/.

Dairy Block & Denver Milk Market

1800 Wazee St., Denver

The Dairy Block is a "micro-district" of restaurants, bars, shops, and a mural-covered alley nestled in the larger LoDo district. There's even a 172-room hotel—The Maven—on the site. Named for the early-20th-century Dairy Windsor Building it partly occupies, the Dairy Block avoids big-scale commercialism and celebrates many "small-batch, iconic, and heritage brands" found only in Colorado. There's really nothing quite like it in Denver. Be sure to check out the giant, colorful murals covering The Alley; local artists created most.

Part of the Dairy Block is the Denver Milk Market—a giant food hall offering a mix of 16 take-out and dine-in restaurants run by Colorado chef Frank Bonanno. There's an eatery "concept" for almost every taste. They range from the Bonanno Brothers Pizzeria and Ghost Tortilla to Ruth's Butchery and Cornicello ice cream. The Stranded Pilgrim offers artisanal beers on tap, Stellar has all kinds of wines, and Moo Bar offers just about every kind of alcohol. This is a great place to fill up while getting a taste of the burgeoning Denver food scene.

Tip #44: Looking to unwind after a day of touring downtown? Stick around for the Dairy Block's "Artists on the Rise" live music series in the summer and fall.

It features up-and-coming Colorado musicians playing in The Alley. Visit the event website at https://dairyblock.com/aotr/ to find out who will be playing and when.

Colorado Rockies at Coors Field

2001 Blake St., Denver

I can remember the excitement in Denver when Major League Baseball (MLB) announced that Denver was awarded one of two expansion franchises in 1991. The Colorado Rockies started playing at the old Mile High Stadium in 1993, and their first season there was so popular that the city decided to enlarge the planned Coors Field in LoDo from 43,000 seats to 50,000 seats. During construction, a 7-foot-wide triceratops skull was discovered on the site, and "Dinger," the dinosaur, soon became the Rockies' official mascot. The mascot is even more appropriate because so many dinosaur fossils have been discovered in the state, including at nearby Dinosaur Ridge.

Coors Field, named by Coors Brewing Company in nearby Golden, was completed by 1995, and the Colorado Rockies have played there ever since. I've been to countless games, and, usually sitting in the upper stands, I've always been struck by the great views of the Rocky Mountains to the north and the Denver skyline to the south. Coors Field has become known as a "hitter's park" because Denver's dry, thin air allows the ball to travel much farther than a ball at sea level. In fact, Coors Field has twice broken the MLB record for most home runs in a season. Despite MLB's efforts to even the playing field, the Rockies still enjoy the best home-field advantage in baseball. Even so, the Rockies have been to the World Series only once, losing to the Boston Red Sox in 2007.

Coors Field is a great place to enjoy a summer afternoon or evening game. In true Denver style, there's an on-site microbrewery—the Blue Moon Brewery at the Sandlot. It's where the Blue Moon Belgian-style wheat beer was invented and makes a fun place to hang out if the game is not going the Rockies' way. And if you want to keep the party going after the game, the many microbreweries of LoDo are only steps away from the stadium.

Tip #45: Every Fourth of July, the Rockies host a fireworks show over the stadium after the game.

If it's not on July 4th itself, it'll be on one of the nights before. It's a fun way to celebrate America's birthday, and you can avoid the traffic jams around other fireworks displays. However, get your tickets early because they're very popular for this date. Visit the team website at https://www.mlb.com/rockies/tickets for the full schedule.

REI Flagship Store

1416 Platte St., Denver

Given that Denver is a magnet for outdoor enthusiasts, it only stands to reason that Recreational Equipment, Inc. (REI) Co-op would establish one of its five flagship stores here. Opened in 2000 just across the South Platte from Confluence Park, the Denver REI flagship store has become a mecca for Colorado's many mountain climbers, campers, skiers, cyclists, and kayakers. The massive 88,000-square-foot store occupies the Denver Tramway Power Co. Building, originally built in 1901.

The historical setting aside, the store is not your typical outdoor gear store. When you first walk in, you notice the spacious "greenroof" populated with aspens, firs, and a 75-foot stream. At the center of the store is a 48-foot-high climbing wall called "the Pinnacle." You soon realize that only 40% of the floor space is devoted to selling products; the remainder is designed to create an experience that inspires people to spend more time outside. I think REI has succeeded in doing that.

In addition to selling almost every kind of outdoor gear imaginable, the member-owned REI Co-op offers all kinds of classes to make the outdoors experience better. They offer everything from navigating the backcountry to rock climbing to canoeing. REI also organizes group hiking and camping trips. It's truly a one-stop-shop for everything outdoors. Check their website at https://www.rei.com/events/p/us-co-denver for upcoming classes and events.

Tip #46: If you're ready for refreshment after spending all day at the REI flagship store, be sure to visit My Brother's Bar on the same block (2376 15th St.).

They serve tasty burgers and beer. One of the oldest bars in Denver, My Brother's Bar is steeped in history and was once a favorite hangout of Neal Cassady, a major figure of the Beat Generation in the 1960s.

Mile High Spirits

2201 Lawrence St., Denver

It can be said that Mile High Spirits is a lot of different things. First and foremost, it's a micro-distillery—yes, Denver just doesn't make beer anymore—that makes whiskies, bourbon, gin, vodka, rum, and tequila on-site. Personally, I like their Fireside bourbon and Denver Dry Gin, but they are all worth a try. They also offer tastings of their homemade spirits and a long list of cocktails made from their spirits. I love the creativity that goes into their concoctions, including the names themselves. Who can resist a "Mexican Firing Squad" made with their own Cuidado Tequila?

But Mile High Spirits is much more than a micro-distillery. Its warehouse-size space has a lounge where you can enjoy post-work drinks with friends (happy hour is 4 pm to 7 pm Tuesday through Friday). It's a music venue and dance space that hosts live music events throughout the year, including "Bloodies and Bluegrass" every Saturday afternoon. It's also a game space with cornhole tables, a picture booth, table toss games, and even bingo nights. Of course, their drinks will make all these activities more fun! For a list of their upcoming events, follow this link: https://www.drinkmhs.com/tasting-room#TR-EVENTS.

Tip #47: If you have a weekday off, you can take a free tour of the Mile High Spirits distillery, where you'll learn how they make all those different kinds of small-batch spirits. And, yes, tastings are included!

Upper Downtown

The area known today as "Upper Downtown" used to be called the Central Business District (CBD) or simply "downtown" by locals. That's how I thought of it when I worked in its office towers while I went to college in the late 1980s and early 1990s. By the 21st century, however, the CBD was eclipsed by its popular and trendy sibling, LoDo. So in an effort to infuse new energy into the neighborhood, the Denver Downtown Partnership decided in 2019 to rebrand the CBD as "Upper Downtown. The moniker "UpDo" hasn't caught on among locals, but maybe that's a good thing. Do we really need another four-letter acronym for a neighborhood? Perhaps lacking the glamor and swagger of LoDo, Upper Downtown is still worth getting to know, however. In addition to Denver's tallest buildings, Upper Downtown has some of Denver's most historic structures and a few of its best-kept secrets to boot.

Centered on where Denver's most important streets come together, Upper Downtown is at the heart of the city. Officially, it's bounded by Lawrence Street on the northwest, 20th Street on the northeast, North Broadway on the east, West Colfax on the south, and Speer Boulevard on the west. But, more simply, I like to think of it as the part of downtown southeast of the D&F Tower. Either way, it's a very walkable part of the city that's easy and worthwhile to explore.

Afternoon Tea at the Brown Palace Hotel

321 17th St., Denver

At the center of Upper Downtown is the elegant Brown Palace Hotel. Since it opened in 1892, it has been Denver's most luxurious hotel. In fact, when it opened, it was a marvel of modern engineering. Guests were amazed by its elevator, telephones, flush toilets, hot showers, and electric lights; every finely appointed room even had a fireplace. Named for its builder, Henry C. Brown (no relation to Denver's most famous resident, Molly Brown), the Brown Palace has hosted every U.S. president except Calvin Coolidge since it opened. The Brown Palace was also famous for hosting The Beatles on their first concert tour in the U.S.

Fortunately, you don't have to be a guest to enjoy some of the Brown Palace's best features. One of them is the daily afternoon tea in the hotel's stunning lobby, an eight-floor atrium adorned with stained glass at the top. If you're a tea snob or simply British, you might call this afternoon ritual of luxury "high tea." However, you will undoubtedly be transported to a more refined era as you sip on your Earl Grey and devour tea sandwiches and scones topped with Devonshire cream imported from England while relaxing to the soft sounds of a live grand piano. It's an experience not to be missed. You can book a table on their website at: https://www.brownpalace.com/dining/restaurants/afternoon-tea/.

If you plan to extend your splurge by staying at the Brown Palace, you will be rewarded with fine cuisine at its three restaurants, crafted evening cocktails, a luxurious salon and spa, and world-class service. You can book a room on the hotel website at https://www.brownpalace.com/, or because the hotel is now owned by Marriott, through Marriott's booking options.

Tip #48: The Brown Palace has on staff its own historian, who offers tours of this historic structure.

Overnight guests can get a tour for $10 every Saturday at 1 pm. In addition, private tours for groups of 1-14 can be booked at other times. Add some spice to the tour by requesting a themed tour, such as a ghost tour or one centered on presidential visits. Ask to see the hotel's artisanal well—the source of its water—and the bee colonies that are the source of its honey. Go to https://www.brownpalace.com/our-hotel/history/hotel-tour/ for booking information.

Tip #49: If you're in Denver during the National Western Stock Show in January, be sure to book an afternoon tea at the Brown Palace. The hotel has a tradition of purchasing the stock show's top-prize-winning steer and displaying him in a pen in the hotel lobby during tea-time!

American Museum of Western Art

1727 Tremont Pl., Denver

Nestled among Denver's skyscrapers and across the street from the Brown Palace Hotel is one of my favorite art museums in Denver, the American Museum of Western Art. It's housed in the historic Navarre Building, built in 1880 as an all-girls school. It changed hands often in its early days, later becoming a gentleman's club and then a "house of ill-repute," or brothel. There was even an underground tunnel connecting the Brown Palace to the Navarre so that "gentlemen" could discreetly visit the brothel!

Today, the remodeled Navarre has a finer purpose, displaying some of the best works of Western art in the Anschutz Collection. (Philip Anschutz is Colorado's richest man and his name appears throughout the city.) There is art created by the 19th century "Hudson School" of landscape paintings, including those by Albert Bierstadt, who could capture the awesomeness of the Rocky Mountains like few others. My favorites are the paintings and sculptures of Frederic Remington, probably best known for his bucking broncos. This is not a big museum, so the artwork is very accessible, and it's a great place to get a feel for Western art.

Tip #50: The American Museum of Western Art has very limited hours, so some advanced planning is needed.

It's only open to the public on Monday, Wednesday, and Friday from 10:30 am to 4 pm. However, group tours for up to 15 people can be arranged on Tuesday and Thursday. Visit this link for more information: https://anschutzcollection.org/group-tours.

Wells Fargo Center & Mile High Center

1700 Lincoln St. and 1700 N. Broadway, Denver

The Wells Fargo Center is probably the most easily recognized skyscraper in the Denver skyline. Locals call it the "Cash Register Building" because its top floors curve together to resemble an antique cash register. In fact, heaters had to be installed on the roof to prevent dangerous slabs of snow and ice from sliding off onto pedestrians below. Completed in 1983, the 50-story icon was first the home of Denver-based United Bank and was known as the United Bank Tower. My mom worked in law offices on the 39th floor of the tower, which afforded her some fantastic views of the city. After a few bank mergers, the building became known as One Norwest Center, and finally Wells Fargo Center.

The Mile High Center is attached to the Wells Fargo Center by a long pedestrian causeway. It was designed by famed architect I.M. Pei as part of a site plan that now includes the Wells Fargo Center. The Mile High Center is considerably shorter than the adjoining tower, but at 23 stories, it was nonetheless the first modern high-rise in Denver when it opened in 1954. Until then, buildings couldn't exceed the height of the 12-story D&F Tower. The Mile High Center is still notable for its giant glass atrium that mirrors the cash-register shape of the Wells Fargo Center's upper floors.

Tip #51: Take a stroll through the Mile High Center's atrium on a sunny day to fully appreciate its grandeur and beautiful design.

Ascend the escalators and cross the pedestrian bridge to the lobby of the Wells Fargo Center, which was remodeled in 2016. There, you'll find a giant 8-story digital screen of changing artwork and a number of other huge paintings and sculptures that bring life to the lobby.

Trinity United Methodist Church

1820 N. Broadway, Denver

Trinity United Methodist Church, completed in 1888, was downtown Denver's first church, and many still consider it Denver's finest church. Others call it one of the best examples of Modern Gothic architecture in the United States. It was the crowning achievement of Denver's first licensed architect, Robert Roeschlaub. The church is notable for its 184-foot spire made of rhyolite, a volcanic material found near Castle Rock, Colorado. Another notable feature is the 1880s-era Roosevelt organ with 4,275 pipes, which makes quite the sound for attendees of Sunday services. It's one of the few Roosevelt organs still in operation. The intricate interior woodwork and stained-glass windows are some of the finest in the city. A 1982 restoration helped keep Trinity United Methodist Church one of the best-preserved historic structures in Denver.

Tip #52: Take a free, self-guided tour of the Trinity United Methodist's impressive interior during regular business hours Monday through Friday.

A free docent-led tour is also available on most Sundays at noon. In addition, guided tours can also be arranged in advance for Wednesdays and Thursdays. Visit the church website at https://www.trinityumc.org/im-new/take-a-tour/ for tour information.

Republic Plaza

370 17th St, Denver

The Republic Plaza building, standing at 717 feet and 56 stories, is the tallest building in Denver, the state of Colorado, and the Rocky Mountain region. It was completed in 1984 on the site of the old Republic Building, which was the tallest building in Denver until the 1950s. Its boxy design and white exterior make it easy to spot among Denver's high-rises. But, perhaps the best thing to be said of its plain design is that its many windows brilliantly reflect the blue sky on a sunny day. I worked on the 42nd floor of the Republic Plaza for two years during college and always enjoyed the magnificent views of the Rocky Mountains and the city. Looking east, some of my coworkers claimed they could see Kansas 150 miles away on a clear day, but I was skeptical they could see that far!

Tip #53: Check out the three-story, marble-clad lobby of the Republic Plaza building.

It's adorned with an "Art in Public Places" exhibit of rotating artwork from Colorado and regional artists. The City of Denver requires all new office buildings to devote one percent of their construction budget to public art displays.

Denver Pavilions Shopping Center

500 16th St. Mall, Denver

Anchoring the southeastern end of the 16th Street Mall is the Denver Pavilions Shopping Center. Opened in 1998 and covering two city blocks, Denver Pavilions replaced the old May D&F department store that went out of business in the early 1990s. I can remember thinking when the May D&F closed—when I worked in the nearby Republic Plaza building—that retail in downtown

Denver was doomed. Fortunately, Denver Pavilions helped make sure that didn't happen.

Today, the three-story, open-air Denver Pavilions is a draw for downtown shoppers and diners alike. It's anchored by a 15-screen United Artists theater (I love the comfy stadium-riser seating) and a Lucky Strike bowling alley. Lucky Strike, with its colorful lighting, expansive bar, and good food, is the modern take on a fun pastime (it's great for parties, too!). The Pavilions also has ten restaurants and eateries, several of which began outdoor service during the pandemic on a blocked-off stretch of Glenarm Place. Large-scale retailers have struggled on the site, but smaller, trendy ones seem to do just fine. Denver Pavilions makes for a fun spot for lunch or a date night.

Tip #54: For one of the best and most easily accessible views of the Denver skyline, go to the Pavilions' third-level plaza between the United Artists theater and the Lime restaurant.

Looking east, you'll see an expansive view of the 16th Street Mall with Denver skyscrapers filling the horizon. It makes for a memorable selfie!

Paramount Theatre

1621 Glenarm Pl., Denver

The historic Paramount Theatre in the heart of Upper Downtown was long considered Denver's most glamourous movie house. When it opened in 1930, 20,000 people came out to witness its premiere on the Denver entertainment scene. Designed in the "Zig-Zag Art Deco" style by Temple Buell, one of Denver's best-known architects, the Paramount recalls the Jazz Age of the 1920s and 1930s. It was equipped with a one-of-a-kind, 1,600-pipe Wurlitzer organ used to create music and sound effects for the silent movies of the day. The organ is one of only two Wurlitzers still in operation today; the other is in New York City's Radio City Music Hall. Organists still do public performances using the Paramount's Wurlitzer.

Today, the 1,865-seat Paramount Theatre is a venue for not only film screenings but theater productions, dance performances, stand-up comedy acts, and lectures by authors on national tours. I can remember attending a lecture there by author James Burke. He was explaining "The Day the Universe Changed," his popular book on the history of science (the book has since been made into a British documentary series). Visit the Paramount's event calendar at https://www.paramountdenver.com/event-calendar/ to see what's coming up and purchase tickets. No matter what you see, you're in for a treat at the beautiful Paramount.

Tip #55: If you have time before or after your show at the Paramount, stroll three blocks to the historic Denver Press Club at 1330 Glenarm Place.

The Denver Press Club, established in 1867, was the first press club founded in the United States. Its 1920s-era lobby is full of the history of journalism. The Denver Press Club is open to the public from 4 pm to 10 pm, Tuesday through Friday. Visit their website at https://denverpressclub.org/ for more information.

Denver Firefighters Museum

1326 Tremont Pl., Denver

The Denver Firefighters Museum, with its collection of firefighting equipment, artifacts, photos, and archival materials, is dedicated to preserving the history of the Denver Fire Department (DFD) and firefighting in Denver. Until it was established in 1979, firefighting artifacts were scattered throughout the city and in danger of disappearing. The DFD's original Station One building, constructed in 1910, was in danger of disappearing under the wrecking ball until the museum's organizers rescued it, restored it, and opened the museum there in 1980.

Today, the Denver Firefighters Museum not only preserves Denver's firefighting history but also promotes fire safety and organizes special events for kids, seniors, and firefighters. Educators can also arrange special visits and field trips. Go to the museum website at https://denverfirefightersmuseum.org/upcoming-events to learn about their upcoming events. The museum is open Tuesday through Saturday, 10 am to 4 pm. For more visitor information, go to https://denverfirefightersmuseum.org/plan-your-visit.

Tip #56: If you're a firefighting fan or firefighter, you can become a museum member for as little as $50/year. You'll gain exclusive, weekly access to the museum, guided tours, and special events throughout the year.

Colorado Convention Center

1555 California St., Denver

Opened in 1990, the "new" Colorado Convention Center (CCC) was part of the slate of major infrastructure and civic projects Denver launched to help revitalize the city. Pope John Paul II hosted World Youth Day at the CCC in 1993, and President Bill Clinton hosted the G-8 Summit there in 1997. Both events helped to solidify Denver's image as a world-class destination. Since then, the convention center has drawn nearly 1 million visitors to the city every year (before the pandemic). In 2004, the CCC underwent a major expansion and opened its own light rail station, giving conventioneers easy access to the Denver metro area. As a result, the CCC has been consistently rated one of the top 10 convention centers in the country, and another expansion, due to be completed in 2023, will undoubtedly increase its appeal to convention planners around the world.

The CCC is perhaps best known to Denverites not for its visitor draw but for the "Big Blue Bear" statue that peers into its glass façade. Officially called "I See What You Mean," the 40-foot, five-ton steel sculpture was designed by Lawrence Argent and installed in 2005. The beloved bear has since become Denver's most popular work of public art and probably its number one selfie spot. The Big Blue Bear is closest to the corner of 14th and Stout Streets.

Tip #57: The Big Blue Bear is not the CCC's only work of art. Go inside the 14th Street entrance to see more giant artworks, such as Mindy Bray's "The Heavy Is the Root of the Light," a 95-foot-wide painting depicting the South Platte River near Confluence Park.

Also, worth seeing is "I Know You Know That I Know" by Sandra Fettingis; it's a 160-foot-long creation that envelops the viewer in a light-filled corridor. To see more examples of art on display, visit the CCC website at this link: https://www.denver.org/meetings/convention-center/public-art/.

Tip #58: If you're looking for a break from your convention or just want to relax at the end of a busy day, saunter across 14th Street to the Hyatt Regency, the second-largest hotel in Denver.

Head up to the 27th-floor lounge to soak in the breathtaking views of the Rocky Mountains while sipping a cocktail. It's one of the best viewpoints of the mountains you'll find in Denver.

Denver Performing Arts Complex

1400 Curtis St., Denver

The Denver Performing Arts Complex (DPAC), a 12-acre, 10-venue site for theater, opera, and music, is the second-largest performing arts complex in the country; only New York's Lincoln Center is bigger. DPAC comprises the nation's first in-the-round concert hall, Boettcher Concert Hall, which is the home of the Colorado Symphony. I saw my first classical music concert there—a performance of Verdi's "Four Seasons"—and I remember being blown away by the sound. The DPAC also includes the Ellie Caulkins Opera House—affectionately called "The Ellie" by locals—the home of Opera Colorado and the Colorado Ballet. In addition, the Helen Bonfils Theatre Complex made up of four separate theaters, hosts many smaller theater productions.

The Buell Theatre, with a seating capacity of 2,885, is by far the largest performance venue at DPAC. Since its sold-out, 10-week *Phantom of the Opera* production in 1991, the Buell has become a favorite national jumping-off point for touring Broadway shows. Some of the most popular of these have included *The Lion King*, *Sunset Boulevard*, *A Chorus Line*, and *The Book of Mormon*. Visit the DPAC's website at https://www.artscomplex.com/events/all to see what's coming next.

Tip #59: If you're visiting the DPAC for a live performance, take a few minutes to see the remarkable 60-foot-tall sculpture "The Dancers" by Jonathan Borofsky.

Its 25,000 pounds of fiberglass and steel dominate Sculpture Park, which is adjacent to the DPAC facing Speer Boulevard. The sculpture symbolizes Denver's exciting performing arts scene, which definitely punches above its weight.

Range Restaurant

918 17th St., Denver

The range restaurant—yes, the "r" is not capitalized—is one of my favorite places to eat downtown. Not only is it in a historic location—inside the elegant Colorado National Bank Building—its food is outstanding. The restaurant describes its food as New American cuisine with an emphasis on "Colorado-inspired" flavors. The bar has many local selections, including beer made in Denver and spirits from the Breckenridge Distillery. The menu changes with the seasons, but starters have included a warm corn and chevre dip with house-made tortilla chips to give you an idea of what's on offer. The entrées often have a Western theme, like rich Colorado bison meatloaf or confit chicken covered with a mouth-watering mole sauce made from Olathe sweet corn. You cannot go wrong with whatever you select.

Tip #60: Be sure to check out the adjoining, marble-clad lobby, which was once the grand lobby for the now-extinct Colorado National Bank.

The building, completed in 1915, has been beautifully restored and added to the National Register of Historic Places; it's now occupied by the boutique Renaissance Downtown Hotel. Sidle up to the lobby's elegant bar for a post-dinner libation and take in the 16-century-old "Indian Memories" murals adorn the lobby.

Gems in the Golden Triangle

As mentioned in Chapter 2, the Golden Triangle is Denver's center of the arts. It was named the first Colorado Creative District in 2016. However, many long-time residents still refer to the area as "Civic Center" because of all the local, state, and federal government buildings here, including the Denver City & County Building, the State Capitol, and the Denver Mint, which we'll explore below. After all, these government buildings predate the magnificent art museums that have appeared in recent decades.

If for some reason, you haven't made it to the Denver Art Museum lately, I highly recommend a visit. It's best not to go when you're pressed for time because there is so much to see in its 12 collections spanning three buildings. In fact, it's probably best to make several visits so as not to wear yourself out. You could easily spend all day there. The museum attracts some of the leading traveling art exhibitions from around the world. I remember that the Norman Rockwell and Claude Monet exhibits from 2020 were especially impressive. Check out the DAM's website for upcoming exhibitions here: https://www.denverartmuseum.org/en/exhibitions#upcoming. You're bound to find something you like!

And if you haven't visited the Clyfford Still Museum yet, it really is a must-see. It's probably the best-regarded art museum in Denver after the DAM. Although the museum houses most of Clyfford Still's work, it's not all on display at the same time, so there are rotating exhibits. Visit the museum's website at https://clyffordstillmuseum.org/exhibitions-events/ to see what's upcoming.

Tip #61: Want to give your kids more exposure to art without boring them? The Clyfford Still Museum has a hands-on art studio where kids of all ages can experiment with a variety of art materials and create their own (Still-inspired?) artwork. The museum also hosts periodic "art crawls" for infants, toddlers, and their parents.

Kirkland Museum of Fine & Decorative Art

1201 Bannock St., Denver

One of the most interesting and unusual art museums in the country, the Kirkland Museum of Fine & Decorative Art, is the Golden Triangle's latest art addition. It opened at its current location in 2018 after moving from a nearby smaller building. Part of the move entailed actually moving the three-story studio and art school of Vance Kirkland—the museum's namesake and principal artist—eight blocks using an ingenious system of remote-controlled articulating wheels. My cousin witnessed the move and said it was fascinating to watch. As a result, Kirkland's studio, now at the heart of the museum, has been fully restored and offers a window into the Colorado transplant's 55-year career of creativity.

Another feature that makes the Kirkland Museum so interesting is its display style. It's one of the few art museums in the U.S. that shows its artwork in a "salon style." This means that rather than grouping similar art pieces into boring glass cases, the many pieces of furniture, glassware, and other decorative items are arranged in various rooms that look like they belong in someone's home. In addition, some rooms contain "comparative collections," which allow the visitor to compare two different styles of fine and decorative art. It really helps bring the art to life.

The Kirkland is open Tuesday through Saturday from 11 am to 5 pm and Sunday from noon to 5 pm. Note that because of the museum's open display style, children under 13 are not permitted inside. Check out their website at https://www.kirklandmuseum.org/visit/plan-your-visit/ for more visitor information.

Tip #62: In addition to hosting traveling art exhibitions, the Kirkland sometimes hosts lecture series to go with them.

For example, 2022 saw an exhibition exploring the link between Frank Llyod Wright's architectural designs and the decorative arts. In addition, the museum hosted a series of expert lectures to expound on the concept. For current and upcoming events, visit the museum's event webpage at this link: https://www.kirklandmuseum.org/exhibitions-events/events/.

Byers-Evans House

1310 Bannock St., Denver

The Byers-Evans House is a beautifully restored Italianate mansion built in 1883 by William Byers, the founder, and publisher of the Rocky Mountain News. (Sadly, the Rocky Mountain News, Denver's first newspaper, went out of business in 2009 after 150 years of operation.) Byers soon sold the mansion in 1889 to William Evans, the son of Colorado's second territorial governor. Members of the Evans family continued to live in the mansion until 1981 when it was donated to the Colorado Historical Society, now known as History Colorado. Some say the Evans still reside there—as ghosts!

Today, the Byers-Evans House has been fully restored to its early 20th-century appearance. Approximately 90 percent of the home's furnishings and decorations originally belonged to the Evans. The Byers-Evans House is also home to History Colorado's Center for Colorado Women's History and hosts displays on the contribution of women to Colorado. Guided tours of the mansion are available Thursday through Monday. Tickets need to be purchased in advance here: https://www.historycolorado.org/center-colorado-womens-history.

Tip #63: The Center for Colorado Women's History hosts periodic fun events at the Byers-Evans House, like garden teas, book club meetings, and virtual tours.

Visit the webpage https://www.historycolorado.org/center-colorado-womens-history to see the schedule of events.

Denver Public Library

10 W. 14th Ave. Pkwy., Denver

The Denver Public Library's huge Central Library building does not look like what most people think of as a library. Instead, it looks like at least a half dozen different buildings combined into one. It reminds me of the New York-New York Hotel in Las Vegas, which combines many replicas of New York's most famous skyscrapers into one structure. The Central Library's 1995 expansion, designed by renowned architect Michael Graves, more than tripled the size of the original Hoyt/Fisher Central Library and blends the two together seamlessly.

In addition to the books and other materials you'd expect at a public library, the Central Library houses two large, unique collections. The Western History and Genealogy collection include 20,000 railroad photos and 75,000 pieces of genealogical information on microfiche. In addition, the Blair-Caldwell African American Research Library holds many works related to Black history in the Western U.S. There's even a replica of the office of Wellington Webb, the first Black mayor of Denver.

Visit the DPL's website at https://www.denverlibrary.org/ for more information on hours, locations, services, and upcoming events. In addition to the Central Library, DPL has 24 branches throughout the City and County of Denver.

Tip #64: Even if you don't want to check out any books, come to the Central Library for its impressive collection of artworks. Go to the fifth floor to see some remarkable paintings of scenes from the Rocky Mountain West.

On the seventh floor is the Vida Ellison Art Gallery, which showcases a revolving collection of contemporary art. Be sure to visit the gallery's balcony, where you'll find one of the best views of Denver's skyline.

Denver Mint

320 W. Colfax Ave., Denver

The Denver Mint is the largest producer of coins in the world. Its 54coin presses produce on average 40,500 coins per minute, which amounts to over 50 million coins per day, or more than 7 billion pennies, nickels, dimes, quarters, half-dollars, and dollar coins per year for circulation. You can tell whether the coins in your pocket were made at the Denver Mint by the "D" stamped on the face of the coin. The Denver Mint also produces commemorative coins and billions of dollars' worth of gold bullion every year.

The history of the Denver Mint can be traced back to the Colorado Gold Rush that started in 1858. So many Colorado prospectors were finding gold that Congress established a branch of the U.S. Mint in Denver in 1862. To operate as quickly as possible, the Denver Mint, in 1863, purchased a private mint already in operation and soon began stamping gold and silver coins. The Colorado Silver Boom of the 1880s further fueled the Mint's operations, and in 1906, the Mint moved into a much larger building, where it continues to operate today.

The Denver Mint has since become one of Mile High City's most popular tourist attractions. Free, 45-minute guided tours demonstrate how the Mint's coins are made, and they show visitors interesting artifacts, like a replica of the first coin press used by the Philadelphia Mint in 1792. Also on display is a rare 1895 "Millionaire Calculating Machine," the earliest example of a mechanical calculator, which the Mint once used to tally gold and silver deposits. .

As of this writing, tours of the Denver Mint have been halted due to the pandemic. To learn when tours will resume, check the Mint's website here: https://www.usmint.gov/about/mint-tours-facilities/denver/visiting-the-denver-mint.

Tip #65: Until the Denver Mint reopens, you can get a virtual tour by downloading and using its app, which is available on iPhone and Android.

Follow the link below to get the app: https://www.usmint.gov/about/mint-tours-facilities/denver/visiting-the-denver-mint.

History Colorado Center

1200 N. Broadway, Denver

The History Colorado Center, which opened in a beautiful new building in 2012, brings to life the history of Colorado. Leaving behind the dusty and staid exhibits of the past, the Center offers many hands-on and interactive exhibits for kids and adults of all ages. The museum at the Center does an excellent job of showing how all the people of what is now Colorado have interacted over the centuries to create the beautiful state we have today. For example, it celebrates the contributions of military veterans to Colorado after World Wars I & II and highlights the considerable achievements of Colorado's large and influential Hispanic community. At the same time, it doesn't sugarcoat terrible events like the Sand Creek Massacre in 1864 or the terror perpetrated by the local chapter of the Ku Klux Klan in the 1920s and 1930s. As a partner of the Smithsonian Institution, the Center welcomes many of the country's most interesting traveling exhibitions. I always learn something new every time I visit.

History Colorado, formerly the Colorado Historical Society, is a nonprofit organization that seeks to preserve and educate the public about Colorado's history. It operates many museums around the state, including the Center for Colorado Women's History at the nearby Byers-Evans House. It also operates the State Historic Preservation Office, the Office of Archeology & Historic Preservation, and the Stephen H. Hart Library and Research Center. To learn more about the History Colorado Center and its upcoming events, visit its website: https://www.historycolorado.org/history-colorado-center.

Tip #66: Want to get more hands-on experience with the history of Colorado? History Colorado offers almost weekly tours and field trips from May to October.

Some activities include walking tours of Denver's Chinatown, Capitol Hill architecture, and Victorian Denver. Other tours go farther afield, like the Castles of Colorado bus tour and a trek to Mesa Verde National Park. For more information, visit the Center's tour webpage here: https://www.historycolorado.org/tours-and-treks.

Civic Center Park

101 W. 14th Ave., Denver

Inspired by the City Beautiful movement, the 12-acre Civic Center Park was designed in the late 19th century to be at the center of civic life in Denver. It was then and still is today. Full of memorials, monuments, and fountains, the park is flanked by the State Capitol on the east, the City & County Building on the west, the Central Business District of Upper Downtown on the north, and the art museums of the Golden Triangle on the south. It's also where Denver's two most important streets, Broadway and Colfax, converge. In addition, civic Center Park is where important political announcements are made and where all kinds of city festivals take place. It has even been featured in a number of Hollywood movies; I most remember the park in scenes from Clint Eastwood's *In the Line of Fire* from 1993. All this has helped Civic Center Park become Denver's only National Historic Landmark.

To see everything the park offers, follow this short walking tour: start on the north side at Voorhies Plaza, the curves of which force

Colfax Avenue to bend around it. The plaza is adorned with the Voorhies Memorial, completed in 1919 to remember the Denver businessman who left his fortune to pay for much of the park's construction. Immediately to the west of the memorial is the Greek-revival style McNichols Civic Center Building, which opened in 1909 as the Carnegie Library. Next, walk south toward the opposite end of the plaza, where you'll find the famous Bronco Buster bronze sculpture. Beyond it is the Greek Amphitheatre, a 1,200-seat performing arts space. Framing the amphitheater is the Colonnade of Civic Benefactors, which Allen Tupper True painted with murals in 1920 to celebrate Denver's civic leaders.

Now turn around and head north along North Broadway. Midway through the block and across the street is the Colorado Veterans Memorial. The red sandstone spire pays homage to over 400,000 Coloradans who've served in American wars. Finish the walking tour by continuing north along Broadway and crossing Colfax Avenue. There, you'll find the Pioneer Monument Fountain, which depicts Kit Carson, a famous frontiersman, trapper, and military man who spent much of his life in Colorado.

Tip #67: Visit Civic Center Park during the spring, summer, and fall for all kinds of fun happenings like concerts, food festivals, and cultural events.

Some events include the Mile High 4/20 Festival in April, which celebrates Colorado's burgeoning cannabis culture. Others include the Cinco de Mayo Festival in May and PrideFest in June. There's also a huge weekly lunch gathering of food trucks on Thursday called Civic Center EATS and free exercise programs during the summer. Check out these websites for the latest schedule of events in the park: https://www.denver.org/listing/civic-center-park/6823/, https://do303.com/venues/civic-center-park.

City & County Building

300 W. Colfax Ave., Denver

Facing the State Capitol across Civic Center Park is perhaps Denver's most beautiful building, the City & County Building. It's

76

the seat of the Denver City Council, the location of the Mayor's Office, and the headquarters for many of Denver's city offices. It's called the "City & County" Building because, by state law, the city of Denver is also one of the state's 64 counties.

The neoclassical City & County Building is probably the most notable accomplishment of Mayor Robert Speer's City Beautiful endeavors of the early 20th century. The building was intended to consolidate city government operations and make them more efficient, but ironically, it took a commission of 40 architects to agree on a design. As a result, it took 26 years for the building to come to fruition. Finally, it was completed in 1932.

Today, you can take a free tour of this architectural beauty during regular business hours. In addition, you'll see the City Council Chambers, the Mayor's Office, many public artworks, and displays about Denver's ten sister cities. Call 720-865-7600 for more information.

Tip #68: If you're in Denver over the holidays, be sure to visit the City & County Building after sunset.

You'll be rewarded with spectacular, colorful lights illuminating the entire exterior. The lights are on for most of December until the end of the National Western Stock Show in mid-January. It's one of my favorite sights in Denver.

Torchy's Tacos

1085 N. Broadway, Denver

Torchy's Tacos is a chain of fast-casual Mexican restaurants from Texas. I like their location in the Golden Triangle because it's fairly unique when it comes to restaurants—it's built out of an old car repair shop. It still even has the upward-sliding doors once used to admit cars needing a fix. The art-deco-inspired bar gives it an appealingly retro feel, too. The menu includes great-tasting Tex-Mex tacos (of course), salads, smoothies, and churros made from scratch. They even have a 3 – 6 pm happy hour with yummy margaritas and sangrias. Torchy's on Broadway makes for a fun relaxing place after a day of touring the Golden Triangle!

Cuba Cuba Café

1173 Delaware St., Denver

If you're looking for an authentic taste of Cuba in Denver, look no further than the Cuba Cuba Café & Bar. It's been owned and operated by a Cuban family since their first location opened here in 2001; they've since opened five other locations in Metro Denver. Occupying a colorful house on the corner of Delaware Street and 12th Avenue in the Golden Triangle, Cuba Cuba, even has its own palm tree outside, which you don't see very often in Denver. They are said to have the largest selection of rum in Denver, and I have to say their mojitos are outstanding. I also think they have the best Cuban sandwiches outside of Miami. Also, be sure to try the delicious ceviche and empanadas.

Tip #69: Even though the original Cuba Cuba has expanded its seating to the patio and lawn, you might wait a long time for a table if you come well after opening time at 5 pm. Cuba Cuba is as popular as ever, but this also makes it a lively and fun place to experience the best Cuban food in Denver.

The Church Nightclub

1160 Lincoln St., Denver

One of Denver's largest and most popular dance clubs is also one of its most interesting because, as you might have guessed, it occupies a former church, a gothic-style Episcopal church built in 1889. The Church Nightclub opened in 1996 and preserved the original building's many stained-glass windows, adding even more color to the lights flashing in sync with the music. Each of the several dance floors has a different kind of music playing on most nights. In addition, the Church's enduring popularity ensures that it regularly attracts some of the best DJs in the West. If you're a dance worshiper, you've got to attend services at The Church. It's open Thursdays, Fridays, and Saturdays from 9 pm to 2 am. Visit the website at https://coclubs.com/church for upcoming DJs and events.

Auraria

What is now the Auraria neighborhood near downtown was the site of one of the first towns in the Denver area. A party from Kansas led by William Russell founded the town of Auraria on the west side of Cherry Creek in October 1858. It was named for Russell's hometown of Auraria, Georgia, also a gold-mining settlement. With thousands of gold prospectors arriving monthly, Auraria grew quickly and for several years eclipsed the size and importance of Denver City on the east side of Cherry Creek. In fact, Auraria was the site of the Denver area's first post office, city hall, saloon, and carpentry shop.

When Colorado was organized into a territory in 1861, local leaders saw the need for a more consolidated city government, and Auraria officially merged with Denver City and the nearby town of Highland. It's said that the deal was sealed over a barrel of whiskey. With the arrival of Denver's first railroad in 1870 at what is now Union Station, many Auraria businesses moved to the opposite side of Cherry Creek, and Auraria's economic importance began to decline. By the late 19th century, it had become a working-class neighborhood and industrial area. Despite its historical importance, the Denver Urban Renewal Authority razed most of the area in the 1960s to make way for new development.

Today, Auraria is best known as the site of some of Denver's largest institutions of higher learning. The Auraria Campus dominates the area west of Speer Boulevard, north of Colfax Avenue, and east of I-25. Fortunately, a few of Auraria's historic buildings have been preserved, and now most of them are offices belonging to the campus. Closer to the South Platte River on the north side of Auraria are large new complexes like the Ball Arena, Elitch Gardens

Theme & Water Park, and the Downtown Aquarium, which we'll cover in more detail below.

Auraria Campus

777 Lawrence St., Denver

The Auraria Campus is home to the largest center for higher education in Colorado. Three "commuter schools"—the University of Colorado Denver (UCD), Metropolitan State University (MSU), and the Community of College of Denver (CCD)—share the campus's facilities. These three institutions enroll more than 55,000 students, the vast majority of whom do not live on campus but rather commute to their respective schools daily.

I was one of those commuter students for four years, attending and graduating from UCD in 1992. Living at home and not paying for student housing sure saved me a lot of money! When I wasn't working a part-time job, I spent most of my school days on campus, either attending classes, reading at the library, or meeting friends at the student union. The campus back then was primarily dominated by non-distinct, low-rise office buildings, but since then, a building boom has added a beautiful new student wellness center, on-site residence halls, and a hotel, and the student union has moved into the historic Tivoli building. So the campus, along with downtown, certainly has changed!

Fortunately, the campus has preserved the few historic buildings that escaped the wrecking ball in the 1960s. One of them is the Emmanuel Art Gallery (1205 10th St. Plaza). Built in 1876 as an Episcopal church, it's one of the oldest remaining structures in Denver. After an influx of Jewish immigrants into Auraria in the late 19th century, the Emmanuel became a synagogue in 1903 and the center of Jewish life in Denver. Later, it became an artist's studio, and today, the small building hosts art exhibits. Also of note on the campus is St. Elizabeth of Hungary Roman Catholic Church (1060 St. Francis Way); built in 1889, it's still a functioning church.

Tip #70: Visitor parking is available at the surface lots and parking garages on 7th Street and 5th Street.

However, parking after 5 pm and on weekends becomes quite expensive for vehicles not registered with Auraria. A good alternative to driving is to use the light rail system; two stations directly serve the campus. The D, F, and H lines serve the Colfax at Auraria station, and the C, E, and W lines serve the Auraria West station.

Ninth Street Historic Park

9th St. Park between Champa St. and Curtis St., Denver

Nestled among campus buildings near the southern end of the Auraria Campus is the Ninth Street Historic Park, a block of beautifully restored Victorian homes and a grocery store. The 13 buildings were built between 1872 and 1906. They're occupied by campus administrative offices today, but in front of each house is an interesting plaque describing the architectural style and who originally lived there. Meticulously maintained gardens and lawns around the houses make the park even more appealing. It's truly like a walk back in time. The park is on the National Register of Historic Places.

Just north of the park on the next block is the Golda Meir House (1148 9th St.), the only surviving U.S. home of the former Israeli prime minister. She moved to Denver in 1913 at age 15 to escape a marriage arranged by her parents. The house was originally located in the Highlands neighborhood, where she attended school for two years. Many years later, the house was moved several times to avoid demolition before finding a permanent site at Auraria. Also on this block is the St. Cajetan's Church, the first Hispanic parish in Denver. Completed in 1925, it became the center of Hispanic life in Denver until the neighborhood was razed in the 1960s.

Tip #71: The Golda Meir House has been restored and transformed into a museum dedicated to the life of Israel's first female prime minister. You can arrange a tour by calling 303-556-3291.

Tivoli Brewing Company Tap House

900 Auraria Pkwy., Denver

The Tivoli Brewing Company Tap House, which opened as a microbrewery in 2015 inside the Tivoli Student Union building, has a long and storied history going back to Denver's earliest years. German immigrant Moritz Sigi founded the Colorado Brewery in the early 1860s; and, in 1870, completed the initial phase of what became the Tivoli Center. After Sigi died in a carriage accident in 1874, John Good bought Colorado Brewery and renamed it the Milwaukee Brewery. He greatly expanded the brewery's operations and added an opera house, bottling company, and a tower building to the site. Good, enamored with the Tivoli Gardens in Copenhagen, Denmark, changed the brewery's name yet again in 1901 to Tivoli Brewing Company. One of the few breweries to survive Prohibition (by making non-alcoholic brews), Tivoli had become one of the country's largest breweries by the 1950s. Sadly, a catastrophic flood in 1965, followed by a prolonged labor strike, caused Tivoli Brewing to go out of business in 1969. At that time, it was the second oldest continuously operated brewery in the U.S.

After falling into disrepair in the 1970s, the Tivoli Center saw new life as a shopping mall in the 1980s. Unfortunately, the mall struggled financially, and in the early 1990s, the Auraria Campus acquired the building and turned it into the student union shared by the campus's three colleges and universities. Today, the building is home to student meeting rooms, the student bookstore, a food court, and of course, the revived Tivoli Brewing Company Tap House, which operates in the brewery's original brewing spaces.

Tip #72: Tivoli makes the full range of ales, lagers, and IPAs on-site, but be sure to try their flagship Helles lager, which pays tribute to the brewery's German roots.

You have to love their other beers, too, even if only for their names, like Mountain Squeeze IPA, Zipline Sour IPA, Get Stuffed Holiday Ale, and Cherry Pie Lager.

Tip #73: Tivoli Brewing offers a one-hour VIP tour and tasting, and for beer die-hards, a two-hour VIP tour and "beer school" where guests can learn how to make their own beer.

Visit the brewpub's website at https://www.tivolibrewingco.com/book-online to schedule a tour.

Denver Nuggets & Colorado Avalanche at Ball Arena

1000 Chopper Cir., Denver

Just north of the Auraria Campus is the 18,000-seat Ball Arena, the home of the Denver Nuggets NBA basketball team and the Colorado Avalanche NHL hockey team. The Colorado Mammoth of the National Lacrosse League also plays here. In addition to sports games, Ball Arena hosts music concerts, professional wrestling, and mixed martial arts events—a total of more than 250 events per year.

The arena opened as the Pepsi Center in 1999, replacing the aging McNichols Sports Arena near the then-Mile High Stadium. The first event at the arena was an acclaimed sold-out concert by Celine Dion. In 2001, the Avalanche (known locally as the "Avs") won their second Stanley Cup Finals at the Pepsi Center (their first championship was in 1996, in their first season in Denver). Sadly, the Denver Nuggets have never made it to the NBA Finals. In 2008, the arena hosted the Democratic National Convention, where Barack Obama was nominated for U.S. president. In 2020, Ball Corporation—the world's largest metal cans and packaging manufacturer headquartered in Colorado—won naming rights and renamed the building Ball Arena.

Tip #74: Coming to Ball Arena for a concert or sports game? Avoid the hassle and expense of parking by arriving at the nearby Ball Arena/Elitch Gardens light rail station, which is served by the C, E, and W lines.

Come early to experience the Breckenridge Brewery Mountain House restaurant, which evokes a 100-year-old mountain cabin. It's accessible from inside and outside the Ball Arena.

Elitch Gardens Theme & Water Park

2000 Elitch Cir., Denver

I can remember the excitement as a kid anticipating a visit to Elitch Gardens; it was the hallmark of summer. The Skee-Ball arcade, the Tilt-a-Whirl ride, and the cotton candy were part of the all-day fun. Back then, Elitch Gardens was much smaller and located in northwest Denver. Elitch's (as most locals call it) started in 1890 when John and Mary Elitch turned their farm on the outskirts of Denver into a small zoo with manicured gardens. After John Mulvihill bought the property in 1916, he and his descendants added attractions like a giant ballroom, a hand-carved carousel, and a Ferris wheel. Elitch's soon became one of the hottest entertainment destinations in Denver, drawing performers like Benny Goodman and Lawrence Welk. Over the years, Elitch's added roller coasters, arcades, and a KiddieLand, and it morphed into an amusement park. In 1995, after 105 years at its original location, Elitch's moved to a new location downtown and constructed many new, large rides.

Today, Elitch Gardens is corporately owned and remains the largest amusement park in Colorado. Thrill-seekers throng to modern, fast-moving rides like the Mind Eraser, Boomerang, and Brain Drain. A new wooden roller coaster called the Twister II is due to open soon. The park has also added a water park with many tall water slides, tube rides, and a wave pool. Several eateries in the park keep kids (and adults) from getting too hungry, too. New rides and attractions are opening all the time, so check the park's website for updated information here: https://www.elitchgardens.com/theme-park/. Elitch's is definitely a fun place to spend a summer day!

Tip #75: Although the Elitch's water park is open only Memorial Day weekend through Labor Day weekend, the Elitch's theme park is open longer, from weekends in late April through weekends in late October.

This makes getting a season pass a good deal if you want to go more than once. The park offers several season pass options starting at $75 per person. Check out this webpage for more information and to purchase passes: https://www.elitchgardens.com/season-passes/.

Children's Museum of Denver

2121 Children's Museum Dr., Denver

Nestled between the South Platte River and I-25, the Children's Museum of Denver at Marsico Campus has become one of Denver's most popular attractions. It draws an average of 450,000 visitors per year. It started very modestly in a converted school bus in 1973. It was so popular that it moved into a permanent building in 1975 and then to its current location in 1984. A 2016 expansion doubled the size of the museum and its grounds to nine acres.

The Children's Museum is oriented to kids aged a few months to eight years, but everyone can have fun here. The museum has 20 hands-on learning exhibits, including ones devoted to water, physics, healthy eating, energy, and creating art. Joy Park is a 30,000-square-foot outdoor activity space. More adventurous kids can climb the 3-story Altitude exhibit or the smaller Box Canyon; these attractions are intended to help kids learn about Colorado's environment. The Children's Museum is a great place to take young ones for the day. It's open Wednesday through Sunday; visit its website at https://www.mychildsmuseum.org/ for more visitor information.

Tip #76: On a nice day, bring a picnic lunch to enjoy Gates Crescent Park, which is adjacent to the south side of the Children's Museum. Kids will love the park's playground, and adults can admire the view of the South Platte River passing in front of the Denver skyline.

Downtown Aquarium

700 Water St., Denver

Next door to the Children's Museum on the South Platte River is the Downtown Aquarium, a 107,000-square-foot facility that has become as much a restaurant as a zoological attraction. Bill and Judy Fleming originally opened it in 1999 as a nonprofit called Colorado's Ocean Journey. The original aquarium highlighted the aquatic wildlife of the Colorado River and the Gulf of California that it empties into. Unfortunately, Colorado's Ocean Journey struggled to compete with a new aquarium at the Denver Zoo and filed for bankruptcy in 2003.

The for-profit Landry's Restaurants soon bought and remodeled the aquarium, installing a giant restaurant and bar with views of the main, one-million-gallon tank. The renamed Downtown Aquarium has more water exhibits highlighting the aquatic habitats of North America, wharves, coral reefs, and the rainforest, among others. Kids will like the "Aquatic Carousel" and 4-D theater that shows 15-minute films with aquatic themes. The aquarium also runs an educational program staffed by volunteers. See the aquarium's website at https://www.aquariumrestaurants.com/downtownaquariumdenver/default.asp for visitor information.

Tip #77: Looking for a unique birthday party experience? The Downtown Aquarium hosts a variety of aquatic-themed birthday experiences that kids and teens will love.

Go to this webpage to learn more: https://www.aquariumrestaurants.com/downtownaquarium denver/birthdays.asp.

RiNo (River North Art District)

As mentioned earlier in this guide, the relatively new RiNo district bills itself as "Where Art Is Made" in Denver. And although there's been a lot of recent gentrifications in this former industrial area, the artsy vibe still fills the air. You can find it by walking down the RiNo Art Alley and marveling at the colorful murals, shopping for home décor at the intriguing co-op Modern Nomad, or enjoying lunch on the artsy tables at Denver Central Market.

RiNo, established by local businesses in 2005 as an arts district, is not an official Denver neighborhood. Instead, it partially overlaps with the official neighborhoods of Five Points on the south (see page XX below), Globeville on the north, and Elyria-Swansea on the northeast. So, technically, it's bounded by Park Avenue on the west, I-25 on the northwest, I-70 on the north, York Street and 40th Avenue on the northeast, and Larimer Street on the southeast. For the purposes of this section, however, we'll cover only RiNo south of the South Platte River and southwest of 38th Avenue because this area is more compact and easier to navigate.

Five Points Neighborhood

Between 20th St. and Downing St., Denver

Five Points is one of Denver's oldest and most historic neighborhoods. It gets its name from the five-point intersection of Welton Street, 27th Street, North Washington Street, and 26th Avenue; it's where a corner of the north-south residential street grid intersects with the northwest-southeast downtown street grid. Five Points was the first Black neighborhood in Denver and was so thriving by the turn of the 20th century that it was known as the "Harlem of the West." This came about because racial segregation was legal in Denver until the 1950s, and Black residents were not permitted to live or stay in most other parts of the city. Even jazz greats like Duke Ellington and Dizzy Gillespie, who regularly performed in the jazz halls on Welton Street, were not permitted to stay in downtown hotels.

With desegregation in the 1960s, prosperous Black residents began moving to other parts of the city and the suburbs, and Five Points started a long decline. By the 1990s, many fine homes were turned into boarding houses, and many businesses were boarded up. However, the arrival of artists in the northern part of Five Points and establishing the RiNo Art District in 2005 began a revival that is still underway. The revitalization of the southern part of Five Points, with its stately former mansions and the Welton Street commercial district, has been slower, but the city has made efforts to speed it up, as we'll see below.

Perhaps the most important landmark in Five Points is the former Rossonian Hotel (2640 Welton St.). Built in 1907 as the Baxter Hotel and renamed the Rossonian in 1929, this modest Beaux-Arts building was Denver's jazz mecca from the 1930s through the 1950s. In addition to Duke Ellington and Dizzy Gillespie, it drew other great jazz performers like Nat King Cole, Billie Holiday, Miles Davis, and Count Basie. Unfortunately, it's been vacant since 1998, but as of this writing, a group of developers has proposed remodeling the Rossonian into a boutique hotel with a jazz hall in the basement.

For more of a taste of Five Points' history, visit the Blair-Caldwell African-American Research Library (2401 Welton Street), a branch of the Denver Public Library. The third floor has exhibits that trace Black history in the West, including replicas of a barber shop built by an escaped slave, the Five Points' Roxy Theater, and the office of Mayor Wellington Webb, Denver's first Black mayor. Also worth a visit is the Black American West Museum & Heritage Center (3091 California St.), originally the Victorian home of Colorado's first black woman doctor, Dr. Justina Ford.

Tip #78: If you're in Denver in June, you're in for a musical treat.

In early June is the Five Points Jazz Festival, which typically draws 100,000 people to celebrate Five Points' jazz heritage in multiple venues. Visit the festival website here: https://www.artsandvenuesdenver.com/events-programs/five-points-jazz-festival/ for more details. Later in June, around June 19th, Denver revived its Juneteenth Music Festival to celebrate the city's Black heritage. The festival includes a parade, concerts, and food and drink stands. Visit their Facebook page for more details here: https://www.facebook.com/JuneteenthMusicFestival/.

Tip #79: Looking for some refreshment after touring Five Points? Try the new Solutions Lounge & Restaurant (2220 California St.) or the charming Pairadice Bar (2209 Welton St.) for some tasty small plates, sandwiches, and lively cocktails.

Larimer Lounge

2721 Larimer St., Denver

Larimer Lounge capitalizes on RiNo's artsy vibe and indeed adds to it. Occupying a remodeled 1892 building, Larimer Lounge brings all kinds of indie, punk rock, and alternative bands to RiNo's already bustling nightlife. Every year, the music venue and bar host dozens of small concerts by bands like Fleetmac Wood, Gift of Gab, and Champagne Drip. Performances on weekend afternoons and weeknights are often open to the 16 and up crowd. Larimer Lounge also hosts periodic free events like bingo nights. Their outdoor patio is great for relaxing after work with a local beer or craft cocktail. Check out their website at https://larimerlounge.com/ for upcoming shows and events.

ReelWorks & Tracks Nightclub

1399 35th St. and 3500 Walnut St., Denver

ReelWorks Denver, known as the EXDO Event Center until 2021, is an independent music and events venue in the heart of RiNo. It occupies a warehouse-size space originally built in 1945 as a tinsmith factory and later became a facility that manufactured film reels used in Hollywood—the new name pays homage to that history. Since the event space opened in the 1990s, it has hosted everything from political rallies and roller-skating nights to concerts and drag shows. In recent years, the 22,000-square-foot venue has attracted big-name DJs for giant dance parties. In 2021, I attended a Pride event that drew 3,000 revelers to watch performers from RuPaul's Drag Race. There's always something fun happening at ReelWorks! Check out the website https://reelworksdenver.com/events/ for upcoming concerts and events.

Speaking of Pride, right next door to ReelWorks is Tracks, Denver's largest gay nightclub (it also has the same owners as ReelWorks). It has the largest LED screen I've ever seen in a nightclub; it covers an entire wall that must be 100 feet long. This only adds to the pulsating lights that envelop the space. Tracks claim to have the biggest light and sound show in the Rocky Mountain region, and I believe it. It has several large dance floors, and when you're ready for a break from dancing, there are several adjoining bars with tables and lounge chairs. If the event is big enough (like with Pride), they will open the connecting doors to ReelWorks and create one super-sized venue! Tracks is open Thursday through Saturday nights and sometimes on Wednesday nights for specific events. To find out about upcoming shows, visit this webpage: https://tracksdenver.com/events/.

Tip #80: Be sure to buy your event tickets early to avoid disappointment. Tracks is very popular with the straight and gay crowds alike, and shows for big events like Pride and Fourth of July weekend often sell out in advance.

Indoor Rock Climbing at Movement RiNo

3201 Walnut St., Denver

Movement RiNo is part of a growing nationwide chain of rock-climbing and fitness centers; it's one of five Movement centers in the Denver area. Occupying a 40,000-square-foot former tin factory, Movement RiNo is one of the chain's largest locations. It has nearly 200 climbing walls to suit every level of rock climber, from beginners to the most advanced. Movement RiNo is the perfect place to build your rock-climbing (or "bouldering") skills before tackling real boulders in Colorado's high country. The center also offers a slew of fitness classes, including Introduction to Bouldering, Alignment Yoga, and Ski Fitness. Movement RiNo is unique in that it has partnered with local food purveyors to create an on-site café, food truck park, and beer garden. Visit their website at https://movementgyms.com/rino/ to learn more about joining.

Mister Oso Restaurant

3163 Larimer St., Denver

Just opened in 2019, Mister Oso has already become my favorite spot for tacos in Denver. Created by chef Blake Edmunds, who made Highland's Senor Bear a success, Mister Oso (oso means "bear" in Spanish) bills itself as a Latin American fast-casual restaurant. It emphasizes Mexican flavors with dishes like authentic cochinita pibil (small pork tacos—my favorite!) and a Mexican-style shrimp cocktail. Mister Oso also has Peruvian roots with its many rotating seasonal ceviches that are mouth-wateringly delicious. Whatever you order, get it with the cauliflower rice, which adds even more scrumptiousness. What's more, the modern interior décor will instantly transport you south of the border.

Tip #81: Come to Mister Oso on a nice-weather day and ask to be seated on the covered patio.

The pillow-lined seats and vine-covered walls make for a cool and comfy spot to have lunch or sip on the house pisco sour during happy hour (3 pm – 6 pm daily).

Bigsby's Folly Craft Winery & Cellar Door

3563 Wazee St., Denver

Bigsby's Folly is on the north side of the railroad tracks in RiNo, a craft winery and cellar door (tasting room). That's right—Denver is not just for beer lovers anymore! Bigsby's Folly, opened in 2016 by Chad and Marla Yetka, brings the "urban winery" concept to Denver. But you might ask, "How can they make wine in Denver?" Bigsby's Folly brings in grapes from California, Oregon, and the

Western Slope of Colorado to make sparkling wine, cabernet sauvignon, pinot noir, rose, and chardonnay wines in small batches on-site (don't be fooled by the small vines out front!).

Bigsby's occupies the former Leymer Engineering Works plant built in 1886, so there's plenty of historical charm and lots of room to make wine, sample tastings, and enjoy great food. Try the huge charcuterie plate, green chili artichoke dip, or wild boar meatballs to accompany your wine. It's a delectable experience in a fun and vibrant atmosphere that you won't soon forget. Visit their website at https://www.bigsbysfolly.com/ to learn more.

Tip #82: Take the "VIP Winemaker for a Day" tour, where you'll get a tour of the winery, learn about winemaking, and actually make your own red blends to go in bottles with your custom-made label. It's a unique experience in Colorado!

Visit the Bigsby's webpage at https://www.bigsbysfolly.com/Experiences for more information on that tour and other experiences they offer.

Capitol Hill

Capitol Hill was once regarded as Denver's ritziest residential neighborhood, and it still is one of its finest. When Henry C. Brown, owner of the Brown Palace Hotel, donated acreage on "Brown's Bluff" (his namesake) in 1868 to build a state capitol building, some of Denver's wealthiest residents realized the appeal of the location. It was high above the muddy streets of downtown, caught nice breezes in summer, and afforded sweeping views of the Rocky Mountains. They started building their mansions just east of the capitol site, and the area soon became Denver's most desirable residential location. James J. and Molly Brown were among those who built their mansions here. Brown's Bluff gradually became known as "Capitol Hill" after the construction of the State Capitol Building began in the late 1880s.

With the Silver Crash of 1893, the Capitol Hill neighborhood began to change. No-longer-rich silver barons turned their mansions into boarding houses or rentals to make ends meet. Later, new construction was often in the form of cheaper apartment buildings or condominiums. By 1930s, Capitol Hill had become a hodgepodge of mid-rise apartments, Art Deco theaters, and subdivided mansions. Its low rents and eclectic architecture attracted artists and bohemians, and it became a favorite spot of the Beatnik Generation of the 1950s. Jack Kerouac and Allen Ginsberg were residents for several years.

Today, Capitol Hill has escaped the wholesale gentrification of other Denver neighborhoods and is still an artsy and quirky place. I like it for the enormous maples and elms—some of the largest trees in Denver—that shade its narrow streets in summer. The neighborhood is officially bounded by East Colfax Avenue on the north, 7th Avenue on the south, North Broadway on the west, and Downing Street on the east. For the purposes of this guide, we'll include the adjacent North Capitol neighborhood on the north side of East Colfax Avenue.

Tip #83: For a nice stroll past some of Denver's finest Victorian and Queen Anne mansions, walk four blocks south of the Molly Brown House & Museum on Pennsylvania Street.

Along the way, you'll see the beautifully restored Capitol Hill Mansion Bed & Breakfast (1207 Pennsylvania St.), built in 1891, and the ornate Paterson Inn (420 E. 11th Ave.), a French Renaissance chateau also built in 1891.

Governor's Mansion

400 East 8th Ave., Denver

At the southern end of Capitol Hill is the Governor's Residence at the Boettcher Mansion, or as locals simply call it, the Governor's Mansion. Built in 1908 by the widow of real estate tycoon Walter Cheesman (after whom Cheesman Park is named), this three-story mansion soon became the talk of high society in Denver. After Mrs.

Cheesman died in 1923, Claude Boettcher, one of Colorado's wealthiest men at the time, purchased the residence and made many additions to it. The Boettcher Mansion later became famous for its lavish parties, including many attended by Charles Lindbergh and one attended by Dwight Eisenhower in 1952. After Boettcher died, his foundation (also named Boettcher Concert Hall) donated the mansion to the State of Colorado to be used as the governor's official residence. Governor Stephen McNichols was the first to occupy it in 1960. Since 1999, however, only one governor has occupied it full-time; the others have chosen to keep their primary residences and use the mansion only occasionally.

The Georgian Revival mansion is known not only for its political importance but for its beauty. Many of the furnishings were originally owned by the Boettchers, who traveled the world to collect artwork and other fine pieces to fill their spacious home. One is the drawing room's President Grant chandelier, which hung in the White House when Grant signed the bill that made Colorado a state in 1876. Other notable pieces include 18th-century Venetian chairs, French chandeliers, and a 16th-century hand-carved Italian baroque credenza. The Palm Room, with its floor-to-ceiling windows, offers extraordinary views of Pikes Peak, 70 miles to the south.

Tip #84: Free public tours of the Governor's Mansion are available but offered only on select days, so some planning is required.

As of this writing, 45-minute docent-guided tours are available only on Wednesdays between 1 pm and 3 pm. Check the mansion website for the latest visitor information: https://governor-residence.colorado.gov/public-tours.

Tip #85: Before or after your tour of the mansion, take some time to visit the beautiful gardens of the adjacent Governor's Park.

Also, just to the east of the Governor's Mansion, on the next block, is the ornate Grant-Humphreys Mansion (770 Pennsylvania St.).

This 30-room grand dame was built in 1902 by James B. Grant, Colorado's third governor, and is used today as a wedding venue.

East Colfax Corridor - Capitol Hill

East Colfax Ave. between Pennsylvania St. and Park Ave., Denver

Drawing on the bohemian vibe of Capitol Hill, the East Colfax Corridor has long been known as a rowdy spot late at night. Home to two major music venues, multiple bars, nightclubs, and many late-night eateries, East Colfax reliably brings out fun-seekers late on Friday and Saturday nights and often during the summer, Thursday through Sunday nights.

The historic Fillmore Auditorium (1510 N. Clarkson St.), built in 1907, is one of the biggest attractions. In its first 63 years, the Romanesque two-story structure alternated between being a theater, roller-skating rink, auto factory, warehouse, and homeless shelter. In 1970, Stuart Green reopened it as the 5,100-seat Mammoth Gardens. The venue soon became nationally famous for billing acts like Jethro Tull, the Grateful Dead, Joe Cocker, Van Morrison, and Linda Ronstadt. An especially loud concert by the Who drew ire from local residents and the police, and the venue was eventually closed down. In 1999, it was remodeled under new ownership and reopened as the more soundproof Fillmore Auditorium. Today, the Fillmore hosts all kinds of concerts by well-known artists. Visit this website to see what's coming up and to buy tickets: http://www.fillmoreauditorium.org/events/.

The smaller but equally historic Ogden Theater is just two blocks east of the Fillmore (935 E. Colfax Ave.). Originally opened in 1919 as a venue for vaudeville acts and shows like those by Harry Houdini, the Ogden was turned into a movie theater in 1937. The Ogden was saved from demolition in 1992 and converted into a 1,600-seat music venue, and it has since hosted concerts by Jackson Brown, Iggy Pop, and The Smashing Pumpkins. Visit their website to see what acts are coming up: https://www.ogdentheatre.com/events.

After the evening shows are over, many revelers head to the bars and nightclubs on East Colfax. One of the more interesting is the 1Up Arcade & Bar (717 E. Colfax), which bills itself as the largest arcade bar in the nation. It has 90 classic video arcade games, 42 pinball machines, and six lanes of Skee-Ball to go along with its 12 beers on tap. Popular among the gay crowd is the upscale X-Bar (629 E. Colfax), which has a large outdoor patio with a bar, and Charlie's (900 E. Colfax), a bar and nightclub that used to be purely Western, complete with line dancing by guys in cowboy hats and boots. Nowadays, it's more of a traditional gay nightclub with drag performances, two dancefloors, and an outdoor patio.

Tip #86: Partying into the early morning hours and having a case of the munchies? Get a slice or two of yummy pizza at SliceWorks (700 E. Colfax, open until 2:30 am) or a confectionary masterpiece at VooDoo Doughnut (1520 E. Colfax, open until 3 am).

Cathedral Basilica of the Immaculate Conception

1530 Logan St., Denver

The Cathedral Basilica of the Immaculate Conception, the headquarters of the Archbishop of Denver, is one of the largest and most beautiful churches in Denver. James J. and Molly Brown, devout Catholics themselves, helped to purchase land for the cathedral in 1902 and see it completed in 1912. The foundation was constructed of granite from Gunnison, Colorado, and much of the interior marble comes from near the town of Marble, Colorado. The leaded stained-glass windows are magnificent, and the cathedral has the most of any church in North America. The cathedral was elevated to the status of minor basilica in 1979, and Pope John Paul II delivered mass here on two days during his visit to Denver in 1993.

Today, the cathedral is the center of Catholic life in northern Colorado. It offers mass three times daily and six times on Sunday. After remodeling the main nave in the 1960s, the church can accommodate up to 900 worshipers.

Tip #87: The cathedral offers periodic free choral performances by rotating groups such as the Rocky Mountain Chamber Singers and the Vittoria Ensemble. They sound truly amazing with the giant organ and soaring acoustics of the 68-foot nave.

Visit their website to learn of upcoming performances: https://www.denvercathedral.org/concerts/.

Uptown Neighborhood

Between E. Colfax Ave. & E. 20th Ave., and between N. Broadway & Downing St.

Officially North Capitol Hill, the neighborhood now dubbed "Uptown" has changed dramatically in the last three decades. When I used to work in office towers on or near Broadway, I would park in one of the many parking lots that dominated this area. Today, the acres of pavement have been replaced by an inviting residential neighborhood full of trees, dog walkers, and bustling eateries.

I'm happy to say that not everything has changed. A fixture of this area since 1976, the Las Delicias restaurant (435 E. 19th Ave.) remains as busy and popular as ever. Although they've expanded into a local chain, the original location here in Uptown still serves up my favorite Mexican food in Denver. And that's saying a lot, considering how many great Mexican restaurants there are in the city! Las Delicias's New Mexico-style smothered burritos have been the go-to Mexican food in my family for decades. In the 2000s, this location expanded and added an open-air second floor that makes a perfect spot to enjoy authentic Mexican cuisine with a margarita on a mild evening. Check out the Las Delicias menu at https://www.lasdeliciasuptown.com/.

Also worth seeking out is Steuben's Uptown (523 E. 17th Ave.), a retro-style diner that specializes in regional American food like New England lobster rolls, Albuquerque green chili cheeseburgers, and Southern-style fried chicken. All of these have been voted the best in Denver, by the way, and the place has been featured on the popular cable show *Diners, Drive-ins, and Dives*. Steuben's commitment to supporting the local community adds to their appeal. Check out their menu at: https://www.steubens.com/uptown-menu/.

Chapter Review

We covered a lot in this chapter, which was all about Downtown Denver and the several historic neighborhoods surrounding it—the greater downtown area if you will. There's a reason this chapter is this guide's biggest: more than half the attractions covered in this guide are in Greater Downtown Denver. That would not be possible if city leaders had not completely reinvented the downtown area in the last 30 years by investing in infrastructure, developing new attractions, and preserving historical treasures. This undoubtedly has helped bring residents back to the city and grow the Denver Metro area as a whole.

Here's a summary of what we covered with some of the highlights from each downtown neighborhood:

- **Lower Downtown**, or LoDo, has been transformed from skid row into Denver's most bustling neighborhood. The microbreweries seen on the LoDo Microbrewery Tour led the way in redeveloping the area. New attractions like the Museum of Contemporary Art, Dairy Block, Coors Field, and Riverfront Park definitely draw people to the area. But then, old favorites like the D&F Tower, Comedy Works, and Skyline Park also continue to enliven the area.
- **Upper Downtown** may not have the caché of LoDo. Still, it retains a lot of what makes Denver special, like the Brown Palace Hotel, American Museum of Western Art, the Denver Pavilions, and the Denver Performing Arts Complex, the second largest in the country.
- The museums of the **Golden Triangle**, like the Clyfford Still Museum, the Kirkland Museum, and the History Colorado Center, bring world-class exhibits to the Mile High City. At the same time, the Denver Mint, Civic Center Park,

and City & County Building show residents that the early 20th-century City Beautiful Movement still makes Denver beautiful today.

- **Auraria** doesn't resemble the Western frontier town that it once was, but the Ninth Street Historic Park and Tivoli Center remind visitors that Denver did, in fact, start here. Today, the Auraria Campus and the big-city attractions of the Ball Arena, Elitch Gardens, Children's Museum, and Downtown Aquarium dominate.
- The **River North Art District**, or RiNo, with the hipster vibe of the Larimer Lounge, only blocks away from the historic "Harlem of the West" Five Points neighborhood, shows the world, again, how Denver can reinvent itself while preserving the best of the past.
- **Capitol Hill** is an eclectic mix of elegant mansions, bohemian music venues, bars, and delicious restaurants. The Governor's Mansion and the Cathedral Basilica suggest an earlier era of grandeur, while the lively East Colfax Corridor pulsates with live music and nightclub dancing on most nights.

Chapter 5: Experience Denver Like a Local – West Side

Overview

Although the majority of Denver's attractions, historical destinations, and good restaurants are in or near downtown, that doesn't mean you won't find some wonderful places to visit on the west side of Metro Denver. In fact, when Denver began to expand in the early 1860s, settlers went westward first, perhaps drawn to the bluffs overlooking the South Platte River or the closer views of the Rocky Mountains. Separated from the rest of the city by the South Platte, westside settlers often had to rely on themselves. For instance, the first bridge across the river was soon wiped out by a flood in 1864. As recently as 1965, floods on the river destroyed bridges and cut off the west side from the rest of the city. This relative isolation has led westsiders to develop a unique and proud identity that persists to this day.

For this chapter, we'll cover the west side of the City of Denver— basically the area west of I-25 to Sheridan Boulevard—and, in Jefferson County, the western suburbs of Arvada, Lakewood, and Golden. Jefferson County has seen tremendous growth since 1970 and has become the fourth-most populous county in the state.

Tip #88: At the risk of sounding confusing, some long-time residents refer to Northwest Denver as "North Denver" or the "Northside."

This goes back to the earliest days of Denver when the few settlers on the west bank of the South Platte were due north of Auraria and downtown. As the city expanded, development west of the South Platte spread southward and became more due west of downtown. For the purposes of this guide, we'll refer to the city west of I-25 and U.S. Highway 85 as "West Denver," which is how most locals think of it today.

The Highlands

When most Denverites refer to "The Highlands," they are usually talking about the neighborhoods of Highland (or Lower Highland), Highland Park, Potter-Highlands, and West Highland. The original town of Highland, on the west side of the South Platte, was one of the three towns that merged to form Denver in 1861 (Auraria and Denver City were the other two). Because of its physical separation from the rest of the city, Highland was slower to develop than other parts of Denver. By the 1870s, however, the area started to take off. In 1875, residents decided to incorporate a new "Town of Highlands" adjacent to Denver between Zuni Street and Lowell Boulevard and between West Colfax Avenue and 38th Avenue. Other Denverites felt like Highlands's residents looked down upon them (those close to the bluffs literally did) and disliked their conservative values that virtually banned liquor licenses, for instance. However, after the 1893 Silver Crash, the town went bankrupt and was annexed by Denver in 1896.

Once again part of Denver, Highlands's residents nonetheless felt neglected by the rest of the city and decided to form their own neighborhood improvement districts. These helped to pave streets, install sidewalks, and expand the streetcar lines all the way to Denver's edge. Later efforts built parks and amenities that attracted more well-to-do residents. After the 1960s demolition of much of Auraria and downtown for "urban renewal," many of those displaced residents, including a sizable Hispanic community, moved into the Highlands. Hispanic residents have left an indelible mark on the Highlands, which still has some of the best Mexican eateries in town.

Today, the Highland neighborhood, which locals usually refer to as Lower Highland (or LoHi) to distinguish it from the other Highlands neighborhoods, is one of Denver's buzziest areas. A lot of gentrification has occurred since the 1990s, but the neighborhood retains a lot of its character, with fine Victorian homes and ornate churches dominating many streets. Of course, it doesn't hurt that close to downtown, you can find some of the best views of the Denver skyline.

Olinger Block

16th St. and Boulder St., Denver

Olinger's Mortuaries, founded in 1890 by John W. Olinger, was the largest and most prestigious mortuary in Denver for more than 100 years. When the famed Western showman "Buffalo Bill" Cody died in Denver in 1917, his body was kept at Olinger's until he was buried on nearby Lookout Mountain. By the 1960s, the giant "Olinger's" sign overlooking I-25 was a fixture of the Denver landscape. Unfortunately, Olinger's was later taken over by corporate interests, and its properties sold off in 2004.

The LoHi developers who acquired the Olinger Block saw fit to keep the giant "Olinger's" sign as a nod to the area's past. In 2008, Paul Tamburello opened Little Man Ice Cream (2620 16th St.) on part of the Olinger site, naming it for his diminutive Italian father, whom many called "Little Man." Today, the 28-foot-high Little Man milk can is as much a part of LoHi as the Olinger's sign. Little Man's homemade ice cream and exotic flavors have become so popular that they've opened five other locations in Colorado.

Adjacent to Little Man Ice Cream is Linger (2030 W. 30th Ave.), an outstanding restaurant offering entrees inspired by food from around the world. It has everything from Dahi Puri from India to Filipino spring rolls to Argentinian dark chocolate cookies for dessert. And with a wink to its former mortuary location, you can try unusual cocktails like the "Corpse Reviver" and the "Mortuary Margarita." To top it off, the views of the Denver skyline are amazing.

Tip #89: Don't feel like a big meal? Head to the lively Linger rooftop patio, with a bar, converted from a 1975 GMC RV and a food truck serving yummy small plates like Wagyu sliders and Korean BBQ tacos.

Williams & Graham Speakeasy

3160 Tejon St., Denver

Williams & Graham opened only in 2011 in LoHi and is my favorite bar in Denver. A throwback to the secretive speakeasies of the Prohibition era, W&G nonetheless has a warm and welcoming vibe. Unfortunately, it's located behind a corner bookstore, so when you first enter the building, you may wonder if you're in the right place. Pretty soon, though, your host will swing open a secret bookcase door and whisk you down a short hall to the bar. You'll immediately be impressed with the leather-covered sofas and 500+ bottles of the finest spirits behind the bar.

The expert bartenders serve up one of the greatest ranges of handcrafted cocktails you'll find anywhere. Some of their classic but uncommon cocktails include a Mezcalero (mezcal, Aperol, white vermouth), a caipirinha (cachaça, lime juice, sugar), and a finely tuned Sazerac (rye whiskey, sugar, absinthe, bitters). The more indulgent can opt for out-of-this-world libations made from rare spirits, like Angel's Envy barrel select bourbon or 18-year-old Macallan scotch. The bartenders will also happily concoct a made-to-order drink for the well indoctrinated. Visit their webpage for the full menu: https://williamsandgraham.com/drinks/.

Tip #90: Given W&G's enduring popularity and small size, reservations are highly recommended. Walk-ups are welcome but can face two-hour waits at the busiest times. Online reservations can be made on OpenTable.

Root Down Restaurant

1600 W. 33rd Ave., Denver

At the eastern edge of LoHi is Denver's best vegetarian-friendly restaurant, Root Down. Built out of a 1950s-era filling station, Root Down opened in 2009 to much acclaim and has been a favorite of LoHi hipsters ever since. It's my vegetarian cousin's favorite restaurant, and it's easy to see why. Internationally-inspired dishes like Indian fried tofu paneer and Colombian arepas keep him going back for more. All of their veggie ingredients come from their own gardens or local farmers. Despite all the vegetarian, vegan, and gluten-free options on the menu, carnivores can still find meaty options like Colorado lamb burger sliders and 36-hour short ribs.

And don't forget to try an inspired cocktail like the Electric Ladyland or the Don Draper. Visit their webpage to see the full menu: https://www.ediblebeats.com/all-menus/root-down.

Tip #91: Ask for a seat on the outdoor patio in nice weather. There, you'll get an unparalleled view of Denver's skyline. Reservations are also strongly recommended and can be made by calling 303-993-4200.

Historic Elitch Garden Theatre

4600 W. 37th Pl., Denver

The Historic Elitch Garden Theatre, recently restored as an active movie house and event space, is one of the last remnants of the Elitch Gardens amusement park at this location in West Highland. The theater, built in 1891 as an open-air playhouse, was part of the original zoological park John and Mary Elitch built to attract city dwellers to what was then the countryside. In 1896, it played the first motion picture in Colorado. After a 1900 remodel, the playhouse could accommodate 1,500 attendees and attracted stage legends like Cecil B. DeMille, Douglas Fairbanks, Grace Kelly, and Edward G. Robinson. With the sponsorship of *Denver Post* heiress Helen Bonfils, the Elitch Theatre became the longest-running summer theater in the U.S.

Declining ticket sales led Elitch's to close the summer theater in 1987. After the amusement park moved to downtown in 1995, the historic building languished and came under threat of demolition. Several preservation efforts faltered until community organizers launched a restoration of the building in 2002. Today, the historic theater hosts movie nights, tours, and community events. Visit their webpage to see what's coming up: https://historicelitchtheatre.org/eventsprograms/.

Tip #92: When visiting the Elitch Garden Theatre, stop at the equally historic Elitch Carousel House (3775 Tennyson St.) about one block to the east. The 1926 structure, which once housed the famous Elitch's hand-carved carousel, has been beautifully restored and today hosts weddings and musical performances.

Lumber Baron Inn & Gardens

2555 W. 37th Ave., Denver

One of the Highlands' most historic buildings, the Lumber Baron Inn in the Potter-Highlands neighborhood, was originally built in 1890 as the 8,500-square-foot John Mouat Mansion. John Mouat was a Scottish immigrant who made a fortune in the lumber and building industries. Unfortunately, he lost the house in the Silver Crash of 1893, and the mansion changed hands many times after that. It alternately became a business school, apartments, a boarding house for Spanish Civil War veterans, and by the 1970s, a center for organic farming. After the death of its owner in 1981, the house fell into disrepair. Later, Walt and Maureen Keller bought the mansion and, after a $1 million renovation, reopened it in 1994 as the Lumber Baron Inn & Gardens.

The Keller's did an amazing job restoring the property to its original floor plan and creating a luxurious bed and breakfast. Its five guest suites on the second floor have 14-foot ceilings, and each ceiling is adorned with a unique design by Bradbury and Bradbury. Each suite also has a Jacuzzi bath, modern WiFi, and beautiful antique furnishings. On the third floor is a grand ballroom with 20-foot ceilings; it's used for weddings, theater productions, and other events. Of course, guests can't miss the beautiful gardens or the English-style afternoon tea. The Lumber Baron Inn makes for a relaxing weekend getaway and a good jumping-off point for exploring Highland. Visit their website for more information or to book a room: https://lumberbaron.com/.

Tip #93: You don't have to be a guest to enjoy the finery of the Lumber Baron Inn.

Every Saturday and Sunday, brunch is open to the public with seating at 10 am and noon. The first-floor restaurant pays homage to the inn's British roots with Scottish toast, an English breakfast, and "Hadrian's Wall." Visit their webpage to see the whole menu and to make a reservation: https://lumberbaron.com/sunday-brunch/.

Historic Elitch Garden Theatre

4600 W. 37th Pl., Denver

The Historic Elitch Garden Theatre, recently restored as an active moviehouse and event space, is one of the last remnants of the Elitch Gardens amusement park at this location in West Highland. The theater, built in 1891 as an open-air playhouse, was part of the original zoological park John and Mary Elitch built to attract city dwellers to what was then the countryside. In 1896, it played the first motion picture in Colorado. After a 1900 remodel, the playhouse could accommodate 1,500 attendees and attracted stage legends like Cecil B. DeMille, Douglas Fairbanks, Grace Kelly, and Edward G. Robinson. With the sponsorship of *Denver Post* heiress Helen Bonfils, the Elitch Theatre became the longest-running summer theater in the U.S.

Declining ticket sales led Elitch's to close the summer theater in 1987. After the amusement park moved to downtown in 1995, the historic building languished and came under threat of demolition. Several preservation efforts faltered until community organizers launched a restoration of the building in 2002. Today, the historic theater hosts movie nights, tours, and community events. Visit their webpage to see what's coming up: https://historicelitchtheatre.org/eventsprograms/.

Tip #94: When visiting the Elitch Garden Theatre, stop at the equally historic Elitch Carousel House (3775 Tennyson St.) about one block to the east. The 1926 structure, which once housed the famous Elitch's hand-carved carousel, has been beautifully restored and today hosts weddings and musical performances.

West Denver

What originally was a small foothold on the west side of the South Platte River in 1861 became a significant part of Denver by the turn of the 20th century. In the 1890s and early 1900s, Denver annexed many square miles west of the South Platte, including the town of Highlands, as we mentioned in the previous section and the small suburb of Berkeley. This took Denver's western boundary to Sheridan Boulevard, and it has mostly remained there ever since. Then, in the 1950s, the construction of I-25 through the South Platte Valley—some long-time residents still call the Denver portion of I-25 the "Valley Highway"—reinforced the bisection of the city into western and eastern halves. For the purposes of this section, we'll cover attractions in Denver west of I-25 that were not already covered in Section 5.2 (The Highlands).

Denver Broncos at Empower Field at Mile High

1701 Bryant St., Denver

Some of my fondest memories growing up in Denver were watching the National Football League's Broncos beat division rivals, both on TV and at their old home of Mile High Stadium. Making it to the playoffs was even more fun. But when the Broncos started going to the Super Bowl on a regular basis in the 1980s, they electrified this sports-crazy city in ways that hardly seem feasible today. Each Super Bowl trip also raised expectations, so when the Broncos failed to win any of those Super Bowl appearances in the 80s, all of Denver seemed to fall into a slump. All that came to an end when the Broncos won back-to-back Super Bowls in 1998 and 1999. The Mile High City at long last felt like a championship city.

Capitalizing on that goodwill, the Broncos owner, Pat Bowlen, persuaded taxpayers to help fund the construction of a new modern stadium to replace the aging Mile High Stadium. In 1999, construction started on parking lots adjacent to Mile High, and in 2001, the Broncos played their first season in the gleaming new, 76,000-seat stadium. Despite public and city opposition, the Broncos sold the stadium naming rights, and the new stadium opened as "Invesco Field at Mile High." Since then, the name has changed a few more times, most recently in 2019 to "Empower Field at Mile High."

Anyone who's lived in Denver for any length of time already knows that the Denver Broncos have an almost deified stature in the city. As such, many fans view the Broncos' home turf at Empower Field as their church. The team is so popular in Denver (and Colorado) that it has sold out every home game since 1970, the longest such streak in the NFL. Season tickets have been sold out for decades as well, and basically, the only way to get them nowadays is to inherit them. Even with the thin mountain air giving players an athletic advantage over opponents, the loudness of the fans (along with the metal flooring of the old Mile High Stadium) has given the Broncos one of the best home-field advantages in the league.

If you really want the full Denver experience and to learn why this is such a sports-crazy city, you have to make it to a Broncos home game. Even if you're not a huge football fan, the excitement of the crowd at Empower Field at Mile High is infectious and not to be missed! For ticket information, visit the Broncos website here: https://www.denverbroncos.com/tickets/.

Tip #95: To get an even deeper appreciation of Broncos history, visit the south side of Empower Field before or after a game, or any time, really.

There you'll find the outdoor Ring of Fame Plaza, which honors the Broncos' greatest players. At the plaza's center is a memorial to legendary former owner Pat Bowlen and an impressive statue of wild horses galloping up a cascading water feature. On the north side of the stadium is the Mile High Monument, which pays tribute to the old Mile High Stadium with original stadium seats, the 27-foot-high "Bucky the Bronco" statue, and other memorabilia. Unfortunately, its hours are more limited, so check the website for details: https://www.denverbroncos.com/stadium/milehighmonument/.

Meow Wolf

1338 1st St., Denver

Meow Wolf Denver: Convergence Station is a four-story immersive art installation that fuses elements of science fiction, modern art, retro themes, and storytelling into one experience. Even that doesn't fully describe what Meow Wolf *is*—I can guarantee it's like nothing you've seen before. Opened in September 2021, Convergence Station is the third Meow Wolf exhibit to open; the original was in Santa Fe, New Mexico, in 2016, and the second in Las Vegas in early 2021. Over four years, it took over 300 artists, including over 100 from Colorado, to create the elaborate and imaginative hands-on artworks that fill its more than 70 interconnected rooms and chambers.

I visited with family in late 2021, and we spent several hours meandering the complex and marveling at the creativity involved. It's truly immersive in that no wall or ceiling is devoid of some kind of sci-fi or surreal expression. We first entered a "transit center" that allowed us to select one of four imaginary worlds to visit first. A "portal" (elevator) quickly whisked us there, and with mouths agape, we started exploring. We encountered the grimy metropolis of C Street, complete with a tiny movie theater showing mind-bending short films and a frozen space castle on Eemia. At times we felt lost, crisscrossing some familiar rooms but then discovering new chambers we had missed before. It's an unforgettable experience that everybody in the family will enjoy.

Tip #96: Meow Wolf has also made room for musical artists with its on-site music venue called Perplexiplex. It hosts small independent musical acts from around the region and makes for a one-of-a-kind concert experience!

Visit this webpage for upcoming performances and to buy tickets: https://tickets.meowwolf.com/events/denver/.

Sloan's Lake Park

Between Lowell Blvd. & Sheridan Blvd., and 17th Ave.& 26th Ave., Denver

One of my earliest memories as a little boy was walking with my family to Sloan's Lake Park; we lived just a few blocks away. At the time, Sloan's Lake seemed huge to me. At 177 acres, it's still the second-largest lake within Denver city limits. I was fascinated by the many ducks, geese, pelicans, and other birds that wade in the shallow lake. Even when the lake froze over in winter, it still seemed densely populated with birds.

Sloan's Lake hasn't always been there, however. When Denver was founded, the area was a dusty bowl traversed by the main road to Golden. Then in 1866, Denver businessman Thomas Sloan staked a large claim to the area in order to start a farm. The story goes that after digging a well to water the farm, he awoke to find much of his land flooded. Evidently, his well had hit an underground spring, and it gushed until the basin was filled. Another spring to the southeast formed Cooper's Lake, which eventually merged with Sloan's Lake. Unfortunately, Sloan didn't live long enough to see a prosperous farm develop; instead, developers in the late 19th and early 20th centuries built a variety of resorts, beaches, and amusement parks around the lake. None succeeded in competing with nearby Elitch Gardens or Lakeside Amusement Park, and by 1923, they were gone, and Denver acquired the land to create a park.

Today, Sloan's Lake and the surrounding park are still a popular destination for city dwellers looking for a taste of nature. Boaters and water skiers (the only Denver lake that allows water skiing)

enjoy the placid waters throughout the summer; there's a small boathouse and boat launch on the north shore. Picnickers will find shady and scenic picnic tables throughout the park, and walkers and bikers use the 2.6-mile loop trail around the lake throughout the year. It's truly a beautiful and relaxing place to spend an afternoon.

Tip #97: Mark your calendar for the Colorado Dragon Boat Festival, which takes place over two days in July at Sloan's Lake.

Typically drawing 150,000 people, it's the largest dragon boat festival in the country, and one of Colorado's largest festivals, period. The festival celebrates Asian history and culture with a colorful dragon boat race, performing arts shows on five stages, an Asian food court, and a traditional lion dance, among other fun activities. Visit this website for more information: https://www.denver.org/things-to-do/spring-summer/festivals-events/colorado-dragon-boat-festival/.

Lakeside Amusement Park

4601 Sheridan Blvd., Lakeside

Lakeside Amusement Park, founded in 1908 on the western edge of Denver, is the oldest amusement park in Colorado and one of the oldest in the country. It has managed to retain much of its old-world style and charm. Lakeside was originally called "White City" and modeled after the 1893 Chicago Columbian Exposition. Ben Krasner, who acquired the park in 1935, remodeled many of the buildings in the Art Deco style and added thrilling new attractions like the wooden Cyclone roller coaster, which is still the park's most popular ride. Located on the shore of Lake Sylvan (now called Lake Rhoda, which Krasner renamed after his daughter), Lakeside took on a resort feel with beaches, a giant indoor swimming pool, and a grand ballroom. In the following decades, Krasner experimented with horse racetracks, a haunted house, bullfights, stock car racing, boat races, and even a 1970s disco; none of it survived. When Krasner's daughter Rhoda took full ownership in 1969, she refocused on preserving the family-friendly and "park of the people" atmosphere her father had long sought.

When I was growing up in nearby Arvada during the 1970s and 1980s, Lakeside had a reputation for being the "poor man's" amusement park. Its low-priced admission tickets were certainly appealing to families who were priced out of the ritzier Elitch Gardens. Many kids insisted the rides were better at Lakeside anyway. And after Elitch's moved to downtown in 1995, Lakeside got a new lease on life. It's still owned by the Krasner family, who regularly invest in the upkeep and new rides. Besides the popular Cyclone, the Wild Chipmunk and Dragon roller coasters continue to draw adrenaline junkies. For the tamer and smaller crowd, there's a KiddieLand, bumper cars, an early 20th-century carousel, and a miniature train ride that goes around the lake. With other westside Denver amusement parks either burned down, out of business or moved away, Lakeside continues to bring out families for a fun time in the summer. For visitor information, go to their website at: https://lakesideamusementpark.com/.

Tip #98: Visit Lakeside in the evening when it comes to life with brilliant lights.

Lakeside's trademark "Tower of Jewels," the 150-foot Beaux-Arts tower at its entrance, is brilliantly lit. It's not covered with the 10,000 white lights it once was, but it still lights up the night sky.

Tip #99: For an impressive view of a Rocky Mountain sunset, visit Inspiration Point Park (4901 Sheridan Blvd., Denver) about two blocks north of Lakeside at sundown.

At about 200 feet higher than downtown, Inspiration Point offers sweeping views of the Rocky Mountains, and the repaved walk to the top makes for a nice evening stroll.

Art-n-Transit on W Line

Light rail West Line between Decatur/Federal and Federal Center stations, Denver and Lakewood

The Art-n-Transit program on the Regional Transportation District (RTD) light rail network has livened up many of its 57 stations. The West (W) Line, which runs from Union Station

downtown to the western suburb of Golden, has some of the system's most interesting works of art and has made them a destination in themselves. Many of the artworks were created by Colorado artists and residents living near the stations. With a three-hour pass that costs only $3, it's easy to hop on and off at each station to peruse the artwork. Visit this RTD webpage for up-to-date rider information: https://www.rtd-denver.com/fastracks/w-line.

Start your light rail art tour at the WLine's Decatur/Federal station near Federal Blvd. and 14th Ave. Located west of the bus gates in the plaza area is the first art installation called "Interdependence," created by Michael Clapper. It's a series of three tall sandstone sculptures imprinted with handprints from neighborhood children. Next, hop on a westbound train and disembark at the Knox Court station; look for a brightly colored retaining wall covered by the work "Illuminating Path." Its many thousands of mosaic pieces were assembled by local students and overseen by artist Jose Aguirre.

Continuing west on the W Line, get off at Sheridan station and go to the east side of Sheridan Bridge. There, you'll find the "Gift of Rain" by John Flemming. This long, dynamic piece made of steel cables and reflective aluminum strips creates the illusion of falling rain, something Denver can usually use more of! Next at Lamar station is "Lakewood Legacy Trees" by Lonnie Hanzon, a series of tall tree-shaped sculptures meant to evoke the agricultural and transportation roots of the suburb of Lakewood. Four stops west at Oak station is "Tread Lightly" by Joshua Wiener, a group of seven colorful steel boats atop "legs" that seem to be taking the boats away. Finally, disembark at the Federal Center station, where you'll find 18 glass installations of varying sizes and colors covering stairs and walkways. The glass pieces change position with the sun throughout the year, ensuring visitors find a dynamic and ever-changing work of art. Visit this webpage to learn more about all the artworks on the W Line: https://www.rtd-denver.com/art-n-transit/rail-stations#W.

Western Suburbs

Once you go west of Sheridan Boulevard, you've crossed from Denver into Jefferson County, Colorado's fourth-most populous county. Jefferson County encompasses most of the bedroom communities that make up Denver's western suburbs. The principal among them, and the ones we'll cover in this section, are Arvada, Lakewood, and Golden. (Westminster is in northern Jefferson County, so we'll cover it in Chapter 8 on the northern suburbs.)

Although Lakewood is purely a suburban creation—it was incorporated in 1969 to prevent Denver from annexing its neighborhoods—Arvada and Golden began as independent towns. Residential growth eventually filled the areas between them and Denver, but their downtowns retain an old-style Western charm you can't find in newer suburbs. The western suburbs, hemmed in by the foothills on the west, were plagued with stagnation in the 1990s and 2000s as residents in search of bigger homes moved to the north or south. Since then, the Denver area's growth boom has infused new life into the western suburbs with new housing, a new light rail line (the Gold Line), and a thriving dining scene.

Casa Bonita Restaurant

6715 W. Colfax Ave., Lakewood

The Casa Bonita Mexican restaurant—made nationally famous by an episode of the animated comedy series *South Park*—is unlike any dining experience you've ever had. Its 85-foot pink tower and 20-foot-high water fountain dominate the Lamar Station Plaza it has occupied since 1974. Once inside the cavernous restaurant, you're immediately transported to 19th-century Acapulco, with cliff divers periodically diving off a 30-foot waterfall into a 14-feet deep lagoon, cowboys getting into shootouts with bandits, gorillas escaping into the dining area, and roaming mariachi bands delighting diners. As a kid, I couldn't wait to go to Casa Bonita because it seemed like such an exotic adventure. The small arcade and hidden caverns behind the waterfall only added to the fun. The cafeteria-style food was pretty terrible–except for the heavenly *sopapillas* (fried dough drizzled with cinnamon and honey)–but as a kid, I didn't care!

Unfortunately, the Casa Bonita in Lakewood–the last of a small regional chain–didn't survive the closures of the pandemic and declared bankruptcy in 2020. Fortunately, Trey Parker and Matt Stone, the creators of *South Park*, bought the property in late 2021 and have plans to reopen a renovated Casa Bonita in late 2022. They've also hired James Beard-nominated chef Dana Rodriguez to revamp the menu with more authentic Mexican cuisine. As a result, residents of the metro area are eagerly awaiting the return of Casa Bonita, arguably one of the most famous attractions in Jefferson County.

Olde Town Arvada

Centered on Olde Wadsworth Blvd. and Grandview Ave., Arvada

Arvada was the site of the first gold discovery in Colorado when, in 1850, Lewis Ralston found gold in the stream that now bears his name. If he and his party weren't already on their way to the California Gold Rush, his discovery might have started the Colorado Gold Rush eight years early. Soon after the Colorado Gold Rush did start in 1858, some farmers were attracted to the good soil and grasses of the Ralston and Clear Creek Valleys and decided to set up a farming community on the ridge between the two. In 1870 new arrival Benjamin Franklin Wadsworth and his neighbor Louis Reno established a town plat of nine square blocks on the ridge. Wadsworth decided to name the new town after his sister's middle name, "Arvada," which also means "fruitful and growing."

Arvada grew slowly until the Denver Tramway Company brought service in 1900, and downtown Arvada soon became a thriving business district with a lumberyard, tannery, blacksmith, and flour mill. A tire manufacturer arrived in 1915. Farming was still the mainstay of the local economy, however. In the 1930s and 1940s,

Arvada became known as the "Celery Capital of the World" for the sweet-tasting Pascal celery produced in the area. A crop disease soon wiped out that distinction, unfortunately. Post-World War II suburban growth reversed Arvada's fortunes, and the population swelled. By 2022, it was the seventh-largest city in the state, with 124,000 people.

To its credit, the city has preserved the original downtown area. When I was growing up six blocks from there, the area seemed old and run-down, with many empty storefronts. The city strove to revitalize the area, and in 1998, "Olde Town Arvada" was designated a National Historic District. City leaders refurbished the iconic water tower– built in 1910 to alleviate water shortages–and converted the old Arva-Pride flour mill, built in 1925–into a museum (5590 Olde Wadsworth Blvd.). They even replaced the aging 1903 elementary school I attended with a modern structure.

Many suburban residents and restaurateurs, tired of the blandness of strip malls and restaurant chains, soon returned to Olde Town with vigor. Today, the area has gained a reputation as a foodie's paradise. Two blocks have been transformed into a pedestrian zone, which only adds to Olde Town's appeal. I love the Colorado cuisine at the Arvada Tavern (5707 Olde Wadsworth Blvd.), built out of a former grocery store, and the School House Kitchen & Libations (5660 Olde Wadsworth Blvd.), built out of an 1882 school house (naturally), and which has one of the largest Western-style bars you'll find anywhere. The Rheinlander Bakery (5721 Olde Wadsworth Blvd.) has fancy cakes and outstanding German pastries. Visit this website to learn more about what to see and experience in Olde Town: https://oldetownarvada.org/.

Tip #100: If you like farmers' markets, you'll love the Arvada Farmers Market in Olde Town Square (5702 Olde Wadsworth Blvd.) every Sunday morning during the summer.

All the local produce is delicious, but the late-summer Colorado peaches are especially delicious. Visit this website to learn more: https://www.arvadafarmersmarket.com/. And save yourself parking headaches by arriving on light rail's newly opened G (Gold)

Line. The square is less than two blocks from the Olde Town Arvada station.

Tip #101: One of my favorite memories as a kid was going to the Arvada Harvest Festival every year in early September.

It was full of food stands, kiddie rides, and lots of excitement in Olde Town's "midway" on Grandview Avenue. Started in 1925, it's one of the oldest festivals in the Denver area. Today, the kiddie rides are mostly gone, but food and craft vendors, a beer hall, and live music more than make up for it! Visit their website for more information: https://arvadaharvestfestivalparade.com/.

Arvada Center for the Arts & Humanities

6901 Wadsworth Blvd., Arvada

The Arvada Center for the Arts & Humanities, which opened on July 4, 1976 (America's bicentennial), is the largest multiple arts center in a single location in Colorado. It's home to three-stage theaters; 10,000 square feet of art gallery space; rehearsal rooms and classrooms for dance, music, and theater; a conference center; an outdoor amphitheater for summer performances; and the Arvada Historical Museum. It was born from the efforts of Arvada school teacher Lois Lindstrom in the early 1970s. She founded the Arvada Historical Society. When she met with the Arvada mayor to propose a history museum for Arvada, the mayor and city council expanded the idea into a facility that would host music, dance, and theater performances for the rapidly growing community. In Arvada, voters in 1974 approved a $3.6 million bond to build the center.

Today, the Arvada Center's theater company is the third largest in the state. In the Black Box Theatre, well-regarded actors perform plays that retell classic tales and new stories with contemporary meanings. Another stage is designed for musical theater, including classic Broadway musicals. The art gallery features exhibitions from Colorado and regional artists. The Arvada Center is also home to the Front Range Youth Symphony and the Colorado Jazz Repertory

Orchestra. The outdoor summer concert series remains as popular as ever (go to the webpage to see what's coming up: https://arvadacenter.org/music-and-dance/summer-concerts). In addition, a dance academy, summer camp for youth, and all kinds of art classes for kids and adults help to fashion the artists of the future. Visit the center's website for more information on everything it offers: https://arvadacenter.org/home.

Tip #102: Don't forget to visit the Arvada Historical Museum on the main level of the Arvada Center.

At the center of the museum is the original Haines log cabin built by settlers in the mid-1870s. The museum also features exhibits from throughout Arvada's history. See this webpage for visitor information: https://arvadacenter.org/galleries/history-museum.

North Table Mountain Park

Between Easley Rd. & Hwy. 93 and 58th Ave. & Hwy. 58, Jefferson County

The hiking trails on North Table Mountain, a giant mesa west of Arvada and north of Golden, are just about the closest mountainous trails to Denver. About two miles long, a mile wide, and 1,000 feet above the surrounding plains, North Table Mountain offers stunning vistas of Metro Denver and the Rocky Mountains. The grass-covered mesa top provides a sanctuary for great horned owls, golden eagles, red-tailed hawks, prairie falcons, prairie dogs, and mule deer. Nesting raptors occupy part of the park, and the Rim Rock Trail that provides access to them is seasonally closed to protect raptor chicks. It really is an escape to nature up there.

You could spend all day hiking the 17.3 miles of trails on North Table Mountain; the North Table Loop Trail, which goes completely around the mesa, is 7.2 miles by itself. However, for a less strenuous hike, I recommend starting at the Mesa Spur on the north side of the park and bearing left on the North Table Loop until you can go right on the Mesa Top Trail. That's a shortcut across the top of the mountain that will save you considerable time. Besides the wildlife, you'll encounter a small pond and a giant radio tower. This hike is a great retreat to nature without driving far into the foothills.

Tip #103: To avoid climbing the steep sides of North Table Mountain at the main trailheads, join the trail system at the Mesa Spur on 58th Ave.

The half-mile spur is a more gradual climb. Also, on a sunny day, bring a hat and sunscreen as there are <u>no</u> trees to provide shade on the trails. Visit the Jefferson County Open Space webpage for more park information: https://www.jeffco.us/1427/North-Table-Mountain-Park.

Colorado Railroad Museum

17155 W. 44th Ave., Golden

An essential outing for train fans of all ages, the Colorado Railroad Museum reminds visitors of the great importance railroads, particularly the pioneering narrow-gauge railroads, played in building Colorado. At the center of the 15-acre complex is an 1880s-style train depot housing exhibits on two levels. First, the railyard contains more than 100 locomotives and railcars used throughout Colorado in the late 19th and early 20th centuries. Some of the rail stock includes an operational 1881 Denver & Rio Grande steam locomotive and an 1890 cog rail steam locomotive that took passengers to the top of Pikes Peak until the 1960s. Also on the grounds is a restored roundhouse where train maintenance is performed.

Perhaps more fun for little kids is the operating scale-model train layout in the museum's lower level. If that's not enough, the museum offers 20-minute train rides in real passenger cars that loop around the grounds. These are available in the winter every Saturday, and in summer, Thursday through Saturday. Visit the museum webpage for more visitor information: https://coloradorailroadmuseum.org/timetable/train-rides/. The museum also has special events like the kids-themed Day Out with Thomas event in September, Polar Express train rides in November and December, and other events throughout the year.

Check this webpage for details: https://coloradorailroadmuseum.org/upcoming-events/.

Tip #104: After working up an appetite and thirst riding trains, head less than a mile up the road to the kid-friendly New Terrain Brewing Company (16401 Table Mountain Pkwy., Golden).

There you can enjoy some refreshing house brews on tap, delicious burgers from the food truck, and on certain days, live music. Check out their website for more information: https://newterrainbrewing.com/home.

Coors Brewery Tour

13th and Ford St., Golden

Perhaps the business that is most identifiable with Colorado is Coors Brewing Company. Adolf Coors and his business partner Jacob Schueler, both German immigrants, founded the brewery on Golden's Clear Creek in 1873. Coors had experience in the brewing business and was attracted to the clear waters and railroad access he found in Golden. As early as 1875, the brewery started offering tours that included samples of its pilsner made from a Czech recipe. In 1880, Coors bought out his partner; by 1890, Coors was the third largest brewery in the country. Prohibition put a damper on growth, of course, but Coors kept the brewery afloat during those years by making porcelain products and malted milk, which he sold to Mars Co. for making candy. Coors beer gained a national following in the 1960s as more Americans, drawn by the fresh air and wide-open spaces, moved to the West in larger numbers. By the mid-1980s, Coors was distributing its beers nationwide and internationally. In 2005, Coors merged with Canadian brewer Molson to form Molson Coors Brewing Company.

Today, guided tours of the Coors Brewery—the largest single-site brewery in the world—are still wildly popular. On the 60-minute tour, you'll learn about Coors' malting, brewing, and packaging processes and a glimpse of historical beer cans, bottles, neon signs, and other memorabilia. At the end of the tour, you'll get a chance to taste three Coors products, such as its traditional pilsner, Coors Banquet, Blue Moon, Keystone, and Miller (from the Molson product line). The last time I took the tour, you could remain in the tasting room for up to three hours so you could try multiple beers. You'll also get to take home a commemorative beer glass. Of course, if you'd rather skip the tour and go straight to the tasting room, you can do that, too. Tours are offered Friday through Sunday by reservation only. Visit this webpage to learn more and to book your tour: https://www.coorsbrewerytour.com/tour-information.

Downtown Golden

Centered on 12th St. and Washington Ave., Golden

Downtown Golden is one of the most charming places in Metro Denver. The famous arch on Washington Avenue says it all: "Howdy Folks! Welcome to Golden, Where the West Lives." It's one of the most photographed signs in Colorado. Nestled in a small valley between South Table Mountain and Lookout Mountain, Golden has been called the "last flat place before the Rockies," and that's pretty much why it was founded here as a mining supply town in 1859. Golden grew so fast that by 1861 it was named the territorial capital. Competition with Denver grew as settlers found more room on the flatlands, and in 1867, the territorial capital switched to Denver. That was probably for the best because that–and Golden's geographical constraints–kept the town's growth in check and helped downtown retain its Old West charm.

That doesn't mean you can't find a lot of modern things to do in downtown Golden. Washington Avenue between Clear Creek and 14th Street is loaded with locally-owned boutique shops selling everything from botanicals to handcrafted art to vintage clothing. In addition, several outdoor gear outfitters will help you get ready for your next ski day, camping trip, or mountain climb. The farmers market that runs June through October on Saturdays showcases Golden's best coffee, pastries, and locally-grown produce (1019 10th St.). Dining options abound, too, from fine dining at the Old Capitol Grill (1122 Washington Ave.)–set in the Colorado Territory's legislative building–to more casual eateries like Woody's Wood Fired Pizza (1305 Washington Ave.). Woody's has some of the best pizza in Metro Denver and, as such, is a favorite hangout for students from the town's Colorado School of Mines.

More things to do include visiting the Foothills Arts Center, which features all kinds of art exhibitions and occupies three historic buildings surrounding a sculpture garden (809 15th St.). You can get a greater sense of how Golden contributed to Colorado's history at the Golden History Museum (923 10th St.). On the other side of Clear Creek from the museum is Golden History Park, which displays original settler log cabins and a one-room schoolhouse. Finally, the American Mountaineering Museum (710 10th St.)–the only museum of its kind in the country–celebrates the history and challenges of mountaineering around the world.

For outdoor enthusiasts, the two-mile loop Clear Creek Trail follows the creek through downtown between Ford Street and the 6th Avenue bridge. It's paved and relatively level. Along the trail is the Clear Creek White Water Park (1201 10th St.), an 800-foot-long man-made course on the creek with boulders, drops, pools, and eddies for proficient kayakers and canoers. Parfet Park (911 10th St.), the city's oldest park, overlooks Clear Creek and makes a nice picnic or resting spot. See the website, https://www.visitgolden.com/, for a list of all the fun things to do in Golden.

Tip #105: Mark your calendar for late July when Golden holds its Buffalo Bill Days to honor William "Buffalo Bill" Cody, the famous Western showman buried nearby Lookout Mountain (see below).

The three-day event includes a parade through downtown Golden, an arts and crafts festival, and a classic car show. Visit the event webpage for more information: https://www.visitgolden.com/event/buffalo-bill-days/14043/.

Lookout Mountain

Lookout Mountain Dr., Golden

Immediately to the west of downtown Golden is Lookout Mountain, aptly named because it has the most panoramic views of Metro Denver. At the top of the twisty and windy Lookout Mountain Drive is the Buffalo Bill Museum and Grave (987 ½ Lookout Mountain Rd.), which memorializes William "Buffalo Bill" Cody. Buffalo Bill was probably the most famous entertainer in America in the late 19th century. His traveling Wild West show, which featured reenactments of the Pony Express, Indian attacks, and stagecoach robberies, brought to life the fading Old West for people all over the U.S. and Europe. After Buffalo Bill died in Denver in 1917, the city acquired 65 acres atop Lookout Mountain as his final resting place. The museum itself helps bring to life the Old West with exhibits like Buffalo Bill's original Stetson hat, a Sitting Bull peace pipe, and the taxidermied head of the last buffalo killed by Buffalo Bill. Visit the website for the latest visitor information: https://www.buffalobill.org/index.html.

A little farther west on Lookout Mountain Drive is the Lookout Mountain Nature Center and Preserve (910 Colorow Rd.). The 100-acre preserve is designed to protect the ponderosa pines and other flora and fauna of the foothill's ecosystem. The site has 2.8 miles of trails, and the 8,000-square-foot Nature Center offers free naturalist-led programs throughout the year. Also on the site is the beautiful 7,000-square-foot Boettcher Mansion, built in 1917 by Colorado millionaire Charles Boettcher as his summer home and hunting lodge. He and his wife called the lavish Arts & Crafts-style structure the "Lorraine Lodge." After a renovation in 2007, the mansion was outfitted to host all kinds of private events, including weddings. Free, self-guided tours are available Monday through Thursday when events are not taking place. See their webpage for details: https://www.jeffco.us/1880/History-Tours.

On the southern end of Lookout Mountain is the Mother Cabrini Shrine (20189 Cabrini Blvd.), which is dedicated to Frances Xavier Cabrini, the Patron Saint of Immigrants. Cabrini, a nun who founded the Missionary Sisters of Sacred Heart in Italy, was sent to Colorado by the Pope in 1889 to care for the state's many new immigrants. She later founded 67 schools, orphanages, and hospitals. It's said that when she was walking on Lookout Mountain in 1904, she touched a rock with her cane, and spring water immediately burst from the spot. The event inspired her to establish a girls' summer orphanage in 1912. To commemorate her good deeds, admirers, in 1954, built a 22-foot statue of Jesus Christ at the highest point on the property. A 373-step trail marked by the 14 Stations of the Cross leads up to the monument. It's a steep but scenic climb, and the stunning views at the top make it worth it. More than 200,000 people make the trek every year. The site also has a museum devoted to Cabrini, a chapel offering daily mass, gardens, and a grotto modeled on the one in Lourdes, France. Visit their website for detailed visitor information: https://mothercabrinishrine.org/.

Chapter Review

This chapter has been about the west side of the Denver Metro area, including the Denver neighborhoods west of I-25 and the suburbs of Jefferson County, including Arvada, Lakewood, and Golden. Westsiders have long had a spirit of pride and independence from the rest of the city, and that is still found in the Highlands neighborhoods especially. Arvada and Golden were also established independently of Denver and have their own long colorful histories.

Below is a summary of the west side attractions we covered in Chapter 5:

- **The Highlands**, including the neighborhoods of LoHi, West Highland, Highland Park, and Potter-Highlands, is one of the oldest parts of Denver. Still, it has seen a revitalization in the last 20 years, making it very popular. The redevelopment of the historic Olinger Block and the addition of the Williams & Graham speakeasy and Root Down restaurant have given the area new flair while remembering the past at the same time. New life has also been infused in old properties like the Lumber Baron Inn and the Historic Elitch Garden Theatre.
- Other parts of **West Denver** feature new modern attractions like the home of the Denver Broncos at Empower

Field, the other-worldly Meow Wolf art installation, and the modern art installed at every light rail station on the West (W) Line. Long-established attractions, including Sloan's Lake Park and the Lakeside Amusement Park, continue to draw and entertain tens of thousands of visitors annually.

- The **western suburbs of Lakewood, Arvada, and Golden** offer some of the most famous and visited attractions in Metro Denver. Casa Bonita in Lakewood, due to reopen in late 2022, is famous for its one-of-a-kind Mexican dining experience. Olde Town Arvada has found new life as a local foodie and festival destination, and the Arvada Center for the Arts & Humanities remains one of the area's most important cultural touchstones. The spirit of the Old West endures in Golden, the former territorial capital, with its Colorado Railroad Museum, Coors Brewery Tour, historic downtown, and Lookout Mountain.

Chapter 6: Experience Denver Like a Local – South Side

Overview

The south side of Metro Denver encompasses South Denver, the small enclave city of Glendale, and the suburbs of Arapahoe County and northern Douglas County. The Denver Tech Center started in the early 1970s as a magnet for technology companies and has spurred growth in South Denver for decades now. Some of Denver's ritziest bedroom communities are in nearby Cherry Hills Village and Greenwood Village. Further south along I-25, technology-fueled growth since the 1990s has led to an explosion of suburban sprawl in cities like Centennial, Highlands Ranch, Lone Tree, and Parker. That has only made traffic worse on I-25, which already seemed bad when I was growing up in Denver in the 1980s.

For this chapter, we'll focus on South Denver, Glendale, and the suburb of Littleton, which has a charming, historic downtown.

South Denver

How one defines "South Denver" is a little squishy, even for long-time residents. Its neighborhoods don't really have a uniform feel, so that makes it more difficult. Neighborhoods like Cherry Creek and Washington Park are generally wealthier than the rest of the city, but it also contains some more bohemian blocks on Santa Fe Drive and South Broadway. I've usually thought of South Denver as the Denver neighborhoods south of downtown centered on I-25 and the stream of Cherry Creek. A more precise way to define the area is the City of Denver south of 6th Avenue, Parker Road, and east of I-25 and U.S. Highway 85. Some residents have an even narrower definition that limits South Denver to the Washington Park neighborhood and the area between I-25 and U.S. 85.

For the purposes of this chapter, we'll take the wider view to cover more ground. We'll also include the independent enclave of Glendale and the Santa Fe Drive Art District, which is actually north of 6th Avenue but doesn't belong to the Golden Triangle area, either.

Art District on Santa Fe

Between W. 7th Ave. and W. 10th Ave., on Santa Fe Dr.

One of Denver's most distinctive areas is the heart of the Lincoln Park neighborhood just south of downtown. The Art District on Santa Fe is the center of Hispanic culture in Denver. Hispanics make up 30% of Denver's population and have been an integral part of the city since its founding. Many buildings in the surrounding Lincoln Park and La Alma neighborhoods are stuccoed, giving the area a New Mexico feel. The Art District on Santa Fe was formed by local artists in 2003 and was designated a Colorado Creative District in 2012. The district is designed to promote the hundreds of Colorado artists whose work is shown in art galleries, dance studios, and theaters in the neighborhood.

One of the pillars of the district is the Su Teatro Cultural & Performing Arts Center (721 Santa Fe Dr.) It's home to the third-oldest Chicano theater company in the U.S., which performs a variety of homegrown productions that speak to the history and experience of Chicanos. Some of the larger art galleries include the Spark Gallery (900 Santa Fe Dr.), Denver's oldest art cooperative, and the Chicano Humanities & Arts Council (CHAC) Gallery (222 Santa Fe Dr.), which showcases Chicano performance and visual art. The Museo de las Americas (861 Santa Fe Dr.) is an art museum dedicated to preserving and exhibiting art from all over the Americas; you can't miss their bright, pink-colored building.

A trip to the Art District on Santa Fe would not be complete without sampling some of its outstanding Mexican cuisine. There are lots of options to choose from, but some of the most popular include El Noa Noa (722 Santa Fe Dr.), which has simple and delicious Mexican food served on a courtyard patio with live mariachi music. For a no-frills option, next door is the El Taco de Mexico (714 Santa

Fe Dr.), which serves up outstanding traditional Mexico City-style tacos. Visit the district's website for a complete listing of places to eat, galleries, and events: https://denversartdistrict.org/.

Tip #106: Perhaps the best way to experience the Art District on Santa Fe is to attend its popular First Friday Art Walk, which is held rain or shine on the first Friday of every month.

Galleries, studios, and event spaces open their doors between 5:30 pm and 9:30 pm so everyone can easily peruse and experience the art. To avoid parking hassles, arrive by light rail at the 10th Avenue & Osage Street station, which is on the C, D, E, F, and H Lines.

South Broadway

Broadway Ave. between 3rd Ave. and Alameda Ave., Denver

The South Broadway business district, which some have started calling "SoBo," is the center of bohemian life in Denver, especially at night. Its calling card is the hipsterish dive bar that doubles as a music venue that can pack a surprising number of people into a small space. These places, combined with many cheap little eateries, keep these seven blocks on Broadway hopping with 20-somethings well into the early morning hours. On weekends, it's one of the liveliest areas in Denver.

That's not to say it has always been like that. South Broadway has undergone several cycles of boom and bust throughout Denver's history. At the turn of the 20th century, it was called the "Miracle Mile" for reinventing itself as a commercial district after many of its large mansions fell into disrepair and were demolished. After another decline in the 1970s, another renewal began in the 1980s when the historic Mayan Theater (110 N. Broadway) was saved from demolition and restored to its former glory. Ornately decorated inside and out with Mayan Indian images, it's now one of the coolest movie theaters in town, showing independent and foreign films on its three screens. The South Broadway Christian Church (23 Lincoln St.) is a castle-like church built in 1891; the benefactor who funded its construction lived in its tower for ten years. Architecturally, it may be the most unique church in Denver.

One of my favorite venues on this strip is Punch Bowl Social Denver (65 N. Broadway), a warehouse-size "foodertainment" center that defies the small, cramped spaces of South Broadway. Founded in 2012, Punch Bowl Social is designed to bring people together in the tradition of Victorian social gatherings around punch bowls. It bills itself as the "Mothership of Fun," with its scratch-kitchen food, craft cocktails, karaoke nights, and many other forms of entertainment like bowling, shuffleboard, Jenga, pool, and old-school arcade games. I had a blast when I visited with my friends. The concept has become so popular that it's expanded to 20 locations around the country, but I dare say the original in Denver is still the best.

Other trendy places to visit on South Broadway include the neon-splashed Blue Ice nightclub and martini bar (22 S. Broadway); Hi-Dive (7 S. Broadway), a funky dive bar and music venue that hosts punk and bluegrass bands from around the country; and Li'l Devils Lounge (255 S. Broadway), a classy and more relaxed bar known for its frozen cocktails and extended happy hour from 3 pm to 8 pm daily.

International Church of Cannabis

400 S. Logan St., Denver

No travel guide on Denver would be complete without mentioning recreational marijuana, or as practitioners like to call the drug, cannabis. Colorado was the second state to legalize recreational cannabis use in 2012, enshrining the practice into its constitution. In January 2014, Colorado became the first jurisdiction in the world to begin legal retail sales of cannabis. Denver has since become one of the top destinations in the world for "cannabis tourism." Dispensaries abound throughout the city—in some areas, on every block. Even though public consumption is not permitted, sometimes you'll still get a whiff of weed smoke walking down a busy street.

Cannabis use is so prevalent in Denver that it shouldn't be surprising that a whole religion around it has emerged. The adherents of "Elevationism" use cannabis as their "sacrament" to meditate and commune with a higher power. They established the International Church of Cannabis in 2017 in an old church built in 1907. Elevationists don't adhere to any dogma; instead, they welcome members from all religious backgrounds.

Even if you're not a cannabis user, the Elevationists' church building makes for an illuminating visit. The interior has been brightly painted, and the patterns on the ceiling are almost psychedelic. The place really comes alive during a free, hourly laser light show called "Beyond." No cannabis consumption is permitted during the show (it's only allowed during spiritual gatherings held by members), so you'll have to imagine what it's like if you're high. Still, this church is quite unique and makes an interesting introduction to cannabis culture in Denver. Visit the church's website for visitor information: https://elevationists.org/.

Cherry Creek

Centered on E. 1st Ave. and S. University Blvd.

The area of South Denver known as "Cherry Creek" comprises some of the wealthiest neighborhoods in Metro Denver and has traditionally been the home of bank presidents, railroad tycoons, and mayors. This area includes Cherry Creek North, the Cherry Creek Shopping Center, the Denver Country Club, and the Country Club Historic District. Denver's well-to-do began building mansions along Cherry Creek as early as the 1880s, and they established the exclusive Denver Country Club (1700 E. 1st Ave.) in 1887 on its banks. However, a massive flood in 1912 wiped out the golf course, so Cherry Creek was dammed and diverted to prevent new floods. Today the creek is channeled entirely under the country club, so its golf games and polo matches can go on uninterrupted.

As Denver's wealthy class grew, so did the Cherry Creek area. The area north of the country club, now the Country Club Historic District, saw many lavish homes and some more modest bungalows built in the early 20th century. Burnham Hoyt, the architect who designed Red Rocks Amphitheatre, designed several of the more prominent homes. One of the more impressive mansions in the neighborhood is the Reed Castle (475 Circle Dr.), completed in 1931 by the widow of Verner Reed, who made a fortune in real estate, ranching, oil, and mining in Colorado's earliest days. Today, this peaceful neighborhood makes for a nice stroll or bike ride along shade-covered streets.

In the late 20th century, the Cherry Creek North neighborhood just to the east became more upscale. Today, pedestrian-friendly 3rd Avenue between University Boulevard and Steele Street feels like Denver's own Rodeo Drive. It's lined with dozens of fashionable boutiques and high-end cafes and restaurants. One of my favorite places to eat is Cocina Colore (3041 E. 3rd Ave.), which offers modern Italian cuisine with an impressive wine list. One block south on 2nd Avenue is even more restaurants, including Cherry Cricket (2041 E. 2nd Ave.), a local icon since 1950 that has make-your-own burgers and a big selection of local beers.

Just south of Cherry Creek North, on the other side of 1st Avenue is the Cherry Creek Shopping Center. It bills itself as "Denver's premier shopping destination," and that's pretty accurate. Originally opened in 1953 and remodeled in 1990, the shopping mall is anchored by the upscale department stores Neiman Marcus, Macy's, and Nordstrom. Among the 100+ smaller stores, you'll find luxury retailers like Louis Vuitton, Rolex, Tiffany, Burberry, and Zara. For the more price-conscious are popular retailers like Banana Republic, Gap, and H&M. Cherry Creek's upscale vibe has helped the mall to remain one of the few successful ones in Metro Denver. See their website for a full list of stores and restaurants: https://shopcherrycreek.com/.

Tip #107: Experience the best that Cherry Creek has to offer during the Cherry Creek Arts Festival, held over three days during the Fourth of July weekend.

The streets of Cherry Creek North are closed to traffic and taken over by hundreds of local artists offering jewelry, ceramics, paintings, photos, clothing, and sculpture. There are also numerous food vendors and stages set up for musical performances. Check out their website for full visitor information: https://cherrycreekartsfestival.org/.

Washington Park

Between Virginia & Louisiana Aves. and Downing St.& Franklin St., Denver

Washington Park—or as locals call it, "Wash Park"-is one of Denver's most delightful and popular parks. Some have likened it to New York's Central Park, even though it's not nearly that big. But, like Central Park, it does offer a wide array of amenities, from a long walking and biking path, boat rentals on a lake, tennis courts, a recreation center, flower gardens, historical buildings, and a broad meadow perfect for summer picnics. It was developed in 1899, and the "Unsinkable" Molly Brown contributed to its design and funding. In addition, the surrounding Washington Park and Washington Park West neighborhoods are some of the wealthiest in Denver, so their well-to-do residents ensure the park is well maintained and safe.

One of my favorite things to do in Wash Park is rent a self-powered foot paddleboat at the historic boathouse and take a leisurely tour of Smith Lake. The lake was created in the late 1860s by John W. Smith, who built a miles-long ditch from the South Platte River to fill the depression and help turn the dusty prairie green. From the boat, it's easy to admire the beautiful boathouse and pavilion, first built in 1913 and restored in the 1980s. On a clear day, you can see all the way to Longs Peak to the northwest and Mt. Evans to the west. It's a relaxing way to spend a fair-weather afternoon!

Glendale

East of Colorado Blvd. and south of Leetsdale Dr.

On the banks of Cherry Creek in southeast Denver is the independent enclave of Glendale. With about 5,000 residents and only a half square mile in area, it's the most densely populated municipality in Colorado. Residents who wanted to remain independent of Denver incorporated the city in 1952. Glendale is dominated by a commercial district at Colorado Boulevard and Virginia Avenue.

Glendale is probably best known in Metro Denver as where late-night partiers go when the bars and nightclubs in Denver close at 2 am on weekends–Glendale allows its bars and nightclubs to remain open until 4 am on Friday and Saturday nights. A Colorado law passed in 2011 allows municipalities to create special entertainment districts that can vary their bars' closing time from the statewide closing time of 2 am. So far, Glendale is the only city in the immediate metro area with a 4 am closing time on weekends.

As a result, places like Shotgun Willie's (490 S. Colorado Blvd.) become packed after 2 am. Shotgun Willie's was founded in 1982 as a "gentlemen's club" (strip club) by owner Debbie Dunafon, and with multiple bars, food service, a cigar room, and 200 "entertainers," its 10,000 square feet makes it one of the largest strip clubs in the country. Another popular nightclub on weekends is El Potrero (4501 E. Virginia Ave.); the name means "the paddock" in Spanish. With a big taxidermied steer head on the wall and a distinctive Western flair, it's easy to see why it's called this. It's the largest gay Latino bar and nightclub in Denver, and its drag shows, big dance floor, and multiple levels draw in big crowds every weekend.

Glendale offers more than just bars and nightclubs, however. Four Mile Historic Park is on its eastern edge (and technically in the City of Denver), which aims to preserve Denver's earliest history. It's run by a nonprofit that touts that this is where "the American West comes to life." The site contains Four Mile House, built in 1859 on the Cherokee Trail as a stagecoach stop, tavern, and inn for travelers headed to Denver City. Four Mile House, so named because it was four miles from Denver at the time, is the oldest surviving structure in the city. It's been converted into a museum that illustrates the plight of early travelers and settlers along the trail. The historic park also showcases an 1860 stagecoach, a reconstructed 19th-century farmhouse, and live farm animals that regularly delight kids. Visit this webpage for visitor information and to purchase tickets: https://www.fourmilepark.org/visit/.

Tip #108: Four Mile Historic Park really does aim to bring Western history to life with many events and educational programs.

One of its most popular is "Way Back Weeks," which educates kids on a different historical theme each week in the summer. The park also offers arts and crafts classes and even "goat yoga" by its resident goats! Go to their website for more information: https://www.fourmilepark.org/.

University of Denver Campus

2199 S. University Blvd., Denver

Just south of I-25 along South University Boulevard is the main campus of the University of Denver (DU), the oldest university in the Rocky Mountain Region. DU is one of the most prestigious private universities in the U.S., and its schools are often rated among the top 20 in the world. Its graduate school of international studies was founded by Josef Korbel, father of Madeleine Albright, the first female U.S. Secretary of State. Perhaps the most distinguished alumnus of the Josef Korbel School of International Studies is Condoleezza Rice, the first Black female national security adviser and U.S. Secretary of State. In addition, the Sturm College of Law and the Daniels College of Business are among the top-rated in the world in their respective fields.

To go along with DU's prestige is its beautiful and historic tree-lined campus, which makes for a great summer walk. The university was originally founded in 1864 as the Colorado Seminary by Colorado's second territorial governor, John Evans. The Colorado Seminary was established downtown, but the rowdy saloon atmosphere was not conducive to learning. Hence, the school moved south to a former potato field in the 1880s and was renamed "University of Denver."

The first building constructed was University Hall in 1892; it's still in use today and is referred to as "Old Main." Other prominent structures include the Mary Reed Building, built in 1932 with funds from Mary Reed, a major benefactor of the university and the builder of a "castle" in the Country Club Historic District. The bell tower of the Buchtel Memorial Chapel is all that remains of the 1917 structure built to memorialize the alumni who died in World War I. The campus is also known for its beautiful gardens and arboretum. Tours of the arboretum can be arranged on this webpage: https://www.du.edu/arboretum/visit/tours.html.

Tip #109: In non-academic circles, DU is best known in the Denver area for its men's ice hockey team.

The DU Pioneers are so good that they've won nine NCAA championships–the most of any university–and most recently in 2022. The excitement of a hockey game at the 6,000-seat Ritchie Center (2240 Buchtel Blvd. S.) on campus is hard to beat. For the schedule and to get tickets during hockey season, go to the Pioneers webpage here: https://denverpioneers.com/sports/mens-ice-hockey.

Tip #110: For a few hours of stargazing on a clear night, visit DU's Chamberlin Observatory (2930 E. Iliff Ave.) in Observatory Park, just a few blocks east of the main campus.

Completed in 1894 by DU's first astronomy professor, the observatory has a 20-inch refracting telescope that illuminates the stars, planets, and astronomical events. The observatory is open to the public on Tuesday and Thursday nights. Go to this webpage for details: https://science.du.edu/physics/chamberlin-observatory.

Points South

In this chapter, we'll cover suburban Denver south of the city. Broadly speaking, this area includes the tony suburbs of Cherry Hills Village and Greenwood Village, the older suburbs of Sheridan, Englewood, and Littleton, and the new sprawling suburbs of Highlands Ranch, Centennial, Lone Tree, and Parker. Although technically part of the City of Denver, we'll also include the area around the Denver Tech Center because it's basically surrounded by the suburbs mentioned above.

Regal Continental Movie Theater

3635 S. Monaco Pkwy., Denver

One of my favorite childhood memories was seeing the new release of *The Empire Strikes Back*, the *Star Wars* sequel, on the giant screen at the Continental Theater. I was blown away by the immersive experience, with the sheer size of the screen and the booming sound. The Continental, which opened in 1966, was the largest movie screen in Denver and the place to see epic movies. Unfortunately, a fire destroyed part of the theater during a 1983 screening of *Return of the Jedi*—but theater staff were able to save the precious celluloid print of the movie (thank goodness!). The theater underwent a major remodel and expansion in 1996 and again in 2008.

Today, the Continental is owned by the Regal/United Artists chain, which has continued to make upgrades to the theater. In addition to the main 869-seat screen—still the largest in Metro Denver and what Regal calls its "RPX" experience—the theater has added an IMAX theater and a "Screen X." For certain showings, the Screen X digitally stretches wide-screen films to cover the walls for an unprecedented 270-degree movie-watching experience. There are seven smaller screens as well. In my opinion, the Continental is still the best place to see an epic movie in Denver. Visit the Regal website for showtimes and to buy tickets: https://www.regmovies.com/theatres/regal-continental-rpx/1130#/buy-tickets-by-cinema.

Fiddler's Green Amphitheatre

6350 Greenwood Plaza Blvd., Greenwood Village

The outdoor Fiddler's Green Amphitheatre is the largest amphitheater in Metro Denver. It originally started in the 1970s as lawn space for workers from the nearby Denver Tech Center to enjoy a lunchtime concert series. It reopened in 1988 as a major 18,000-person capacity concert venue; it has 7,500 fixed seats, and the rest of the space remains an open lawn. After undergoing several name changes during the 2000s, the venue reclaimed its original name in 2013. Today, Fiddler's Green is open from May to September and hosts medium-sized musical acts like James Taylor, Backstreet Boys, and an interesting collaboration between the Colorado Symphony and Boyz II Men. Combined with fantastic views of the Rocky Mountains, Fiddler's Green is a great place to enjoy an evening concert during the summer. Go to their website to see the upcoming schedule and to purchase tickets: https://www.fiddlersgreenamp.com/.

Tip #111: Arrive early before your concert to check out Marjorie Park (6331 S. Fiddler's Green Cir.) next door to Fiddler's Green.

The park, operated by the Museum of Outdoor Arts, has a permanent exhibition of 40 outdoor sculptures and hosts visiting exhibits as well. The permanent collection includes several Alice in Wonderland-themed sculptures by Harry Marinsky and "The Etruscan Chimera." Visit the website for a description of everything in the park: https://moaonline.org/marjorie-park/.

Historic Downtown Littleton

Main Street between S. Santa Fe Dr. and Rio Grande St., Littleton

Littleton is one of those Denver suburbs that started as an independent town and, over the decades, grew with Denver to form one large urban area. Littleton was founded in 1862–only four years after Denver–by Richard Little, an irrigation engineer from New Hampshire who decided to buy farmland and settle in the area. He and other settlers built the Rough and Ready Flour Mill in 1867, which became a catalyst for the town's steady growth. The town was incorporated in 1890 and remained agriculturally based until the 1950s and 1960s, when Martin Marietta established rocket-building facilities nearby. As a result, the town grew rapidly and today has 45,000 people.

Because of Littleton's early founding and preservation efforts, the city's Main Street retains an "Old West" and small-town charm that's hard to find in other suburbs. Main Street is full of historic structures that have been converted into fashionable boutiques, lively coffee shops, and delicious cafes and restaurants. For example, Cafe Terracotta (5649 S. Curtice St.) serves refined eclectic cuisine from around the world in a delightful Victorian house. If you're staying until evening, don't miss the local plays and art gallery at the Town Hall Arts Center (2450 Main St.), which occupies a beautifully restored 1920 municipal building. Historic Downtown Littleton is a nice place to spend a relaxing day.

Tip #112: To avoid traffic and parking hassles, plan to arrive by light rail on the C or D Lines.

Disembark at the Littleton-Downtown station, where you'll also get a chance to see the original 1875 Littleton train depot; the stone building has been converted into a coffee shop. Main Street is just a block and a half north via Prince Street.

Cherry Creek and Chatfield Reservoirs

I-225 & Parker Rd. and C-470 & S. Wadsworth Blvd.

The two largest state parks in Metro Denver surround two of the area's largest lakes, Cherry Creek and Chatfield Reservoirs. The 880-acre Cherry Creek Reservoir was formed in 1950 when the U.S. Army Corps of Engineers completed the 140-foot-tall earthen Cherry Creek Dam to finally bring disastrous floods on the creek to an end. Today the surrounding state park is a paradise for outdoors-lovers. It can become crowded in summer with boaters, swimmers, jet skiers, picnickers, bird watchers, runners, cyclists, horseback riders, and campers. However, at more than 3,300 acres and with 35 miles of multi-use trails, the park can usually accommodate everybody. The northwestern side of the reservoir has the Cherry Creek Marina & Yacht Club with boat launches, and the northeastern side has imported sand for a day at "the beach." Visit this website for visitor information: https://cpw.state.co.us/placestogo/Parks/cherrycreek .

The 147-tall Chatfield Dam was built on the South Platte River in response to the disastrous 1965 flood that wiped out nearly all Denver's bridges over the South Platte. The 1,423-acre Chatfield Reservoir was formed after the completion of the dam in 1975. Today, the surrounding Chatfield State Park is a magnet for boaters, swimmers, campers, and bird watchers. I remember going to the man-made beach every summer; it was the closest thing I had to an ocean growing up in Denver! With over 200 species of birds, including bald eagles, inhabiting the park, the Audubon Society established the Audubon Center at Chatfield State Park as a nature education center. Go to this webpage for full visitor information: https://cpw.state.co.us/placestogo/Parks/Chatfield.

Tip #113: Just to the west of Chatfield State Park is the satellite location of the Denver Botanic Gardens called Chatfield Farms (8500 W. Deer Creek Canyon Rd.).

The 700-acre Chatfield Farms is a native plant refuge and working farm with miles of trails and several historic buildings. It's a great place to take the kids or just to appreciate nature. See the website for visitor information: https://www.botanicgardens.org/chatfield-farms.

Roxborough State Park

4751 Roxborough Dr., Douglas County

My favorite state park in Metro Denver is Roxborough State Park, about 25 miles south of Downtown Denver. The park is known for its dramatic red sandstone formations, which are part of the same geologic feature that forms Red Rocks Amphitheatre and the famous Garden of the Gods near Colorado Springs. They are all eroded parts of the Dakota Hogback that run along the Rockies' eastern side from Wyoming to New Mexico. The park was established in 1975, and in 1980, it was designated a National Natural Landmark.

In addition to the red rock formations, I love the park for its 14 miles of easy-to-steep trails, overlooks of the city and plains below, brilliant wildflowers in spring and summer, and wildlife like mule deer. It could easily take you all day to hike each of the eight trails. The park also contains several archeological sites that reveal Native Americans inhabited the area from 10,000 years ago to as recently as 1850. Artifacts like Clovis arrowheads and broken pottery are on display in the visitor center, which is a good place to learn more about the ancient cultures that once lived here. Visit the park's website to get visitor information and learn about all there is to do: https://cpw.state.co.us/placestogo/parks/Roxborough.

Tip #114: On weekends during spring, summer, and fall, plan to arrive early in the day to ensure you get a parking spot. The parking lots are fairly small and fill up quickly during these popular times to visit.

Chapter Review

Over the last several decades, the south side of Denver has seen the most explosive growth of any part of the metro area. The Denver Tech Center and huge companies like Lockheed Martin have been some of the leading magnets of growth. As a result, I-25, the main southern corridor, experiences horrendous traffic jams that can double or triple the time it takes to get around. Fortunately, several light rail lines can help you avoid the worst of it if you plan ahead. That said, the south side of Denver has many attractions that make venturing to the area worth your time.

Here's a summary of the main points of interest we covered in this chapter:

- **South Denver**, which we defined as the City of Denver south of about 6th Avenue, has many cultural and historical attractions as well as vibrant commercial districts. The Art District on Santa Fe, with its many art galleries, performance venues, and Mexican restaurants, is the center of Hispanic life in Denver. South Broadway is a raucous and fun commercial district that draws a young, hipsterish crowd on weekends. The wealthy and historic neighborhoods of Cherry

Creek offer many upscale experiences, and Washington Park is an all-around fun and relaxing place to spend an afternoon. The enclave of Glendale has both a vibrant nightlife and the Four Mile Historic Park. The shade-lined University of Denver campus showcases more history, an arboretum, an observatory, and the best place to catch an ice hockey game in Denver.

- **The southern suburbs** of Littleton, Greenwood Village, and Douglas County offer even more fun things to do, like catching an epic movie on the area's biggest movie screens or an outdoor concert in summer. Downtown Littleton's Main Street is full of modern boutiques, cafes, and coffee shops occupying restored historic buildings, which give it an Old West and small-town charm. Outdoors enthusiasts like boaters, swimmers, hikers, wildlife watchers, and campers will be in paradise at Cherry Creek, Chatfield, and Roxborough State Parks.

Chapter 7: Experience Denver Like a Local – East Side

Overview

The east side of Denver stretches from east of downtown through northeast Denver and the huge suburb of Aurora onto the windswept plains around Denver International Airport. The growth of Denver beyond City Park was slow due to the distance from railroads and major water sources like Cherry Creek and the South Platte River. Even farther east in Adams and Arapahoe Counties, no appreciable urban development occurred until the early 20th century. Some growth was spurred by the arrival of military installations like Fitzsimmons Army Hospital (1918), Lowry Air Base (1938), and the Army Air Corps' Buckley Field (1941). Only in the 1970s and 1980s did people begin moving east in large numbers, partly due to the growing scarcity and high land prices to the west. Today, the City of Aurora, just to the east of Denver, is Colorado's third-largest city, with nearly 400,000 residents.

For this chapter, we'll cover basically the northeast quadrant of Metro Denver, which includes east-central and northeast Denver, much of Aurora, and Commerce City.

East Denver

Most Denverites think of "East Denver" as that part of the city centered on Colfax Avenue east of the Capitol Hill neighborhood. East Denver includes middle-class to upper-middle-class neighborhoods like Cheesman Park, City Park West, City Park, Congress Park, Park Hill, and Montclair. In Chapter 2, we covered the area's biggest attractions, City Park and the Denver Museum of Nature & Science. For this section, we'll focus our attention on Cheesman Park and other interesting things to see and do in or near City Park.

Cheesman Park

Between E. 8th & 13th Aves. and Humboldt St.& Race St., Denver

At the center of the Cheesman Park neighborhood is, naturally, Cheesman Park. This 81-acre green expanse began as a cemetery in 1858, in Denver's first year of existence. On the eastern edge of town at the time, it became Denver's main cemetery in 1873. As other cemeteries were established, few new burials occurred here after 1880, and the area became overgrown. Nearby residents sought to convert the eyesore into a park, and the families of those buried there began transferring graves to other cemeteries. By 1893, some 5,000 bodies remained unclaimed, so the city hired a contractor to move them. Unfortunately, the contractor's work was abysmally sloppy, and the mayor canceled the contract without hiring anyone new to finish the job. Park construction continued nonetheless, and it opened in 1907 with perhaps thousands of graves covered over. The new park was named after Walter Cheesman, a leading businessman and city founder, whose heirs built a neoclassical pavilion in the eastern part of the park to memorialize him.

Cheesman Park's design was inspired by the City Beautiful Movement, which was popular in Denver around the turn of the 20th century. One of the park's hallmarks includes a figure-eight layout of the main road in the park. The park underwent a restoration in the 1970s, which converted the crumbling base of the pavilion into a stepped lawn with fantastic views of the Rockies. New flower beds and a rose garden were also installed to complement the existing reflecting pools. Today, the park has a popular picnic area, and you can usually find many sunbathers relaxing on the green on a warm summer afternoon.

Tip #115: Cheesman Park is a favorite hangout of Denver's large LGBTQ+ community. As such, the park is the starting point of the annual PrideFest parade that stretches 14 blocks to Civic Center in late June.

Typically drawing 100,000 participants and spectators, it's one of the largest gay parades in the country. Visit the website https://denverpride.org/ for more information.

Denver Botanic Gardens

1007 York St., Denver

On the east side of Cheesman Park is the Denver Botanic Gardens, one of the finest natural spaces in the city. The 23-acre gardens were once the Catholic section of the Mt. Prospect Cemetery that included what is now Cheesman Park. After Cheesman Park was constructed, this area became the Mount Calvary Cemetery. Seeing the cemetery in disuse and disrepair in the 1950s, the founders of the Colorado Forestry and Horticultural Association began planting a variety of gardens there to spruce it up. They soon convinced the city to relocate the graves and establish the Denver Botanic Gardens.

Today, the gardens have the largest collection of temperate plants in North America. Its seven collections include a xeriscape or desert garden that was the first demonstration xeriscape garden in the world. In addition, the Boettcher Memorial Tropical Conservatory houses all manner of tropical plants and flowers, including an impressive collection of orchids. The garden grounds also boast a large and delightful lily pool, or "aquatic garden," a Japanese garden with water features, and a garden devoted to native Colorado plants and flowers. The gardens are beautifully laid out and often highlighted with stunning art pieces from the likes of Dale Chihuly and Alexander Calder. The landscape is always changing, so it's worth coming here at least once a year to stroll the many gravel pathways. For visitor and event information, go to the garden's website: https://www.botanicgardens.org/.

Tip #116: Come to the Denver Botanic Gardens at lunchtime to enjoy a delicious light meal on the shaded patio of the Hive Garden Bistro.

Try one of the salads made from ingredients grown at the gardens or Chatfield Farms. It's the perfect place to relax and recharge after touring the extensive gardens.

Tip #117: Come to the Denver Botanic Gardens on summer weekends for evening concerts at its sunken amphitheater; it often hosts some big musical names.

On Monday and Wednesday evenings in summer, a variety of local ensembles produce relaxing music throughout the gardens for their "Evenings al Fresco." See this webpage for upcoming performances and details: https://www.botanicgardens.org/events/special-events/music-gardens.

East Colfax Corridor - City Park

E. Colfax Ave., between Park Ave. and Colorado Blvd.

As you go east of the Capitol Hill neighborhood on East Colfax Avenue, you'll encounter another interesting stretch of this major commercial corridor. If it seems like Colfax Avenue goes on forever, it almost does–at 49.5 miles, it's the longest street in the U.S. However, this part of East Colfax south of City Park has some interesting attractions. Foremost is the famous Tattered Cover Book Store (2526 E. Colfax), a Denver institution since 1971. The original store opened in Cherry Creek North and eventually grew into a four-story behemoth. But with intense online competition and falling book sales, the Tattered Cover was forced to close its flagship store and move into this much more modest location in 2006. It's in the renovated historic Lowenstein Theater, which makes an interesting place to find a new read and dig into it at their on-site cafe. There are six other Tattered Cover locations in Metro Denver. Visit their website for more information: https://www.tatteredcover.com/.

Right next door is another Denver institution, Twist & Shout Records (2508 E. Colfax), probably the largest remaining record store in Denver. It certainly has the largest collection of new and used vinyl records, and with occasional live music, it's a fun place to shop for music. On the same block is the Sie FilmCenter (2510 E. Colfax), an independent movie theater showing artsy, hard-to-find films. It's run by the nonprofit Denver Film, which sponsors the Denver Film Festival in November, an increasingly well-regarded and important festival among film aficionados. Many of the festival screenings are at the Sie FilmCenter. Go to their website to see what's playing: https://www.denverfilm.org/.

About a half-mile east on Colfax is the Bluebird Theater (3317 E. Colfax), a historic concert hall that first opened in 1913 as a vaudeville theater. It was later converted into a movie house, but during the Great Depression, other uses were found for it. In 1994, new owners remodeled it into a 500-person capacity music hall, and it has since hosted well-known acts like Ed Sheeran, Macklemore & Ryan Lewis, Scissor Sisters, Twenty One Pilots, and Snow Patrol. The standing-room-only balconies give this classic theater a cozy and more intimate feel than other concert halls in Denver. Visit their website for upcoming shows and tickets: https://www.bluebirdtheater.net/. And just down the street is the smaller Lost Lake Lounge (3602 E. Colfax), a dive bar with retro decor, and a stage hosting indie musical performances.

Tip #118: If you're looking for a post-shopping or pre-concert bite to eat, then you must try the Route 40 Cafe (2550 E. Colfax) next to the Tattered Cover.

This retro roadside diner with modern American eats and cocktails pays homage to the long history of Colfax Avenue (designated as U.S. Route 40) as one of Denver's most important vehicular arteries. There's a small museum inside with interesting artifacts dating to the early 20th century.

Denver Zoo

2300 Steele St., Denver

Occupying the center of City Park is the 80-acre Denver Zoo, one of the most highly regarded zoological parks in North America. It is known for its breeding programs that help maintain endangered species and for its innovative animal enclosures. The zoo was founded in 1896 when an orphaned black bear was gifted to the Denver mayor, and when he had trouble managing it, he gave it to the manager of City Park to raise. In its early days, the zoo was a hodgepodge of mostly Colorado fauna, including bison and elk. Then, in 1907, the zoo became the first in the U.S. to move its animals from barred cages to natural enclosures that are still one of its hallmarks. Finally, with public support in the mid and late 20th century, the Denver Zoo expanded dramatically to include animals and plants from all over the world.

Today, the Denver Zoo features a 7-acre Primate Panorama that includes Monkey Island, which is inhabited by capuchin monkeys. The 10-acre Elephant Passage is big enough to house 12 elephants– 8 of them bulls–and allows zookeepers to study the behavior of bull elephants in herds. Also noteworthy is Tropical Discovery, which includes a giant aquarium and tropical exhibits containing animals like vampire bats, frilled lizards, and poison dart frogs. Predator Ridge houses African lions and spotted hyenas. Kids especially love hands-on exhibits like the seasonal Stingray Cove, where they can touch and feed stingrays. The excellent and ever-expanding exhibits draw 2 million visitors a year, making the Denver Zoo the most visited attraction in Colorado. Check out the zoo website for information on all of its exhibits and how to visit: https://denverzoo.org/.

Tip #119: Keep an eye out for the zoo's Free Days, which happen seven times a year and require signing up for a lottery give-away. Also popular are the "Bring a Friend for Free" (BFF) days. Visit this webpage for more information: https://denverzoo.org/free-days/.

Tip #120: If it's not too cold, visit the zoo for Boo at the Zoo on Halloween–kids love it.

Also popular are the Zoo Lights in December, when the zoo grounds are decorated with brilliant, animated lights depicting the zoo's animals. Check this webpage for times and dates: https://denverzoo.org/events/.

Gates Planetarium

Inside the Denver Museum of Nature & Science in City Park, the 125-seat Gates Planetarium has been delighting astronomy fans for decades. I can remember being dazzled as a little kid by the star shows on the domed ceiling. As a teenager, I loved the planetarium's laser light shows timed to popular rock music. In 2016, Gates was remodeled with a full-dome eight-projector projection system that is truly dazzling. Gates Planetarium continues to offer mind-expanding experiences about the universe, including shows on black holes, weather on other planets, and how the solar system was formed. Some of the shows are in Spanish as well. For showtimes and tickets, visit the planetarium's webpage here: https://www.dmns.org/visit/planetarium/.

Wings Over the Rockies Air & Space Museum

7711 E. Academy Blvd., Denver

Wings Over the Rockies is the largest air and space museum in Colorado, located on the grounds of the former Lowry Air Force Base on Denver's eastern edge. It was founded in 1994 when Lowry Air Force Base–in the process of closing down–transferred a hangar to volunteers to start the museum. Today, the 182,000-square-foot hangar displays over 50 air and spacecraft and several permanent exhibits. Out front, you can't miss the gigantic B-52 Stratofortress bomber built in 1955. Inside are other historic military aircraft like a UH-1 Huey helicopter, a supersonic B-1A Lancer bomber, and F-4 Phantom and F-14 Tomcat fighters. On the futuristic side is an HL-20 Dream Chaser, a concept space shuttle designed to take astronauts into low-Earth orbit. *Finally, Star Wars* fans will love the full-size replica of an X-Wing starfighter.

Other interesting exhibits include a look at Colorado's many astronauts; a memorial to Jack Swigert, a Colorado Apollo astronaut and congressman-elect; an Apollo moon rock; and two flight simulators that visitors can try out. Go to the museum's website to learn more about the exhibits and upcoming events: https://wingsmuseum.org/.

Points East & Northeast

To the east of Denver is Aurora, a vast expanse of suburban subdivisions and shopping centers that have attempted to develop a city center with some success. The area north of Aurora and I-70 was mostly empty prairie until the City of Denver, in 1988, annexed 54 square miles of neighboring Adams County to build Denver International Airport, which locals simply call "DIA." Since the new airport opened in 1995, development has taken off in this once-barren area. Likewise, the suburb of Commerce City, just to the north of Denver, was once primarily an industrial center of oil refineries, grain elevators, and warehouses. Now it has grown rapidly into a bedroom community, with subdivisions stretching well north of the industrial area and east of I-76, almost to the boundaries of DIA.

This section will cover northern Aurora, Dick's Sporting Goods Park, the Rocky Mountain Arsenal National Wildlife Refuge, the new Gaylord Rockies resort near DIA, and the airport itself.

Stanley Marketplace

2501 Dallas St., Aurora

Located next to the grounds of the old Stapleton Airport, Stanley Marketplace was originally built in 1954 as an airplane hangar for Stanley Aviation. The innovative company, once the largest employer in Aurora, built ejection seat systems for the military. After the Stanley manufacturing plant closed in 2007, the hangar was redeveloped, and it reopened in 2016 as a multitenant, multi-level marketplace. Today it is open to over 50 native Colorado businesses, including restaurants, eateries, clothing, home stores, exercise spaces, a beer hall, and even a Tattered Cover Book Store for kids. The Denver Biscuit Company is hugely popular and serves out-of-this-world breakfast and brunch fare. My favorite spot is

Rosenberg's Bagels; their lox and cream cheese on a freshly-baked chewy bagel tastes like it came directly from New York. Don't forget to go upstairs for more shopping in unique boutiques or for yummy ice cream. The Stanley Marketplace is a fun place to spend a leisurely half day. Check out their website for more on what they offer: https://www.stanleymarketplace.com/.

Tip #121: Don't feel like leaving? You can turn your half day into a full day by staying until the evening for their many special events.

These include movie nights, Latin dance classes, trivia nights, and live music on their back patio from June to September. Visit this webpage to learn more about what's coming up: https://www.stanleymarketplace.com/happenings/.

Colorado Rapids at Dick's Sporting Goods Park

6000 Victory Way, Commerce City

Denver is one of the few cities in North America to have a team from all five of the top professional sports leagues, a testament to Denverites' love of sports. The Colorado Rapids soccer team became the latest addition when it was a founding member of Major League Soccer (MLS) in 1995. The Rapids played their first season in 1996 and soon found success, advancing to the finals in their second year. They went on to win their only MLS Cup in 2010.

The Rapids played their first 11 seasons at the old Mile High Stadium, then the new Invesco Field at Mile High, where the Broncos football team plays. Consistently high ticket sales seemed to justify the construction of the Rapids' own stadium, and in a deal with Commerce City, an 18,000-seat stadium was built and opened in 2007. Dick's Sporting Goods won a 20-year contract for the naming rights to the stadium. It was a good investment because the stadium regularly draws near-capacity crowds for some exciting soccer matches. For the team's schedule and tickets, go to their website: https://www.coloradorapids.com/tickets/.

The stadium has also hosted a number of international matches for friendlies and World Cup qualifiers. Less often, the park is converted into a music venue for major concerts from the likes of the Dave Matthews Band, Guns N' Roses, and Green Day.

Rocky Mountain Arsenal National Wildlife Refuge

Between 56th & 96th Aves. and Quebec Pkwy. & Pena Blvd., Adams County

This 25-square-mile national wildlife refuge is located east of I-76 between Commerce City and Denver International Airport. It occupies the site of the former Rocky Mountain National Arsenal, a chemical weapons manufacturing facility that operated from 1942 until 1985. After its closure, environmental tests revealed that the area was extremely polluted and marked for a massive cleanup. It was also found to contain many species of wildlife, so the Rocky Mountain Arsenal was designated a national wildlife refuge in 1992. Unfortunately, the cleanup occurred in stages and wasn't completed until 2010, costing $2.1 billion.

Today the Rocky Mountain Arsenal Wildlife Refuge is home to 332 species of wildlife, including at least 16 bison, brought from Montana as part of a pilot program to restore bison to the area. The refuge is open to visitors, who can drive the 11-mile Wildlife Drive or walk the 20 miles of trails to view the wildlife. It's not hard to spot the imposing bison and mule deer that stand out against the short-grass prairie. Smaller species include coyotes, raccoons, ferrets, and prairie dogs, and bald eagles and raptors can be spotted in the trees near several small lakes and streams. The new visitor center, opened in 2011, highlights many of these species and their importance to the local ecosystem. Only eight miles from downtown Denver, the refuge makes for a fun and engaging encounter with nature. Visit the refuge's website for more information: https://www.fws.gov/refuge/rocky-mountain-arsenal.

Tip #122: To get even more out of the self-guided Wildlife Drive, listen to the U.S. Fish & Wildlife Service's podcast as you go along.

It describes various wildlife viewpoints, old homesteads, man-made lakes, and other features along the route. The drive takes about one hour. You can find the podcast at this link: https://truthandlegend.com/rmanwr-audio-tour.

Gaylord Rockies Resort & Convention Center

6700 N. Gaylord Rockies Blvd, Aurora

Rising out of the plains near Denver International Airport is the gigantic Gaylord Rockies Resort & Convention Center, which opened only in 2018. This 85-acre development includes a 1,400-room hotel, half a million square feet of meeting space, five restaurants, a world-class spa, and a very sizable water park for the exclusive use of guests. Many hotel rooms and suites offer stunning views of the snow-capped Rocky Mountains on a clear day. The Arapahoe Springs Water Park will delight kids and adults alike with a heated lazy river that's open most of the year, water slides, a heated pool that is open all year, and a sunbathing deck. The Great Lodge will instantly transport you to a luxurious ski chalet, even though the resort is a good 27 miles due east of the mountains. The Gaylord, aligned with Marriott Hotels, is on the expensive side, but if you're in the mood to splurge on a "staycation," this is a relaxing place to do it.

Jeppesen Terminal at Denver International Airport

8500 Peña Blvd., Denver

I can remember back when Denver International Airport, or "DIA" as locals call it, was under construction in the late 1980s and early 1990s, so many people decried the project as a "boondoggle" or "white elephant." It's true that the $4.8 billion airport faced huge cost overruns, long delays in opening, and a malfunctioning automatic baggage handling system. But all that was soon forgotten when air travelers were met by the impressive white-peaked roof of the Jeppesen Terminal (named after aviation safety pioneer Elrey Jeppesen). The roof, meant to evoke the snow-capped peaks of the nearby Rockies and the teepees once used by Native Americans in the area, has become a widely-recognized symbol of Denver. Passengers were also amazed by the cavernous interior of the terminal and the underground train system connecting the terminal to the three concourses. DIA was a modern breath of fresh air compared to the cramped and dingy old Stapleton airport.

DIA, the second largest airport in the world by land area, was designed to relieve the frequent and crippling traffic jams at Stapleton that occurred during snowstorms. Not only has this "boondoggle" made national air traffic flow much better, but it has also brought an estimated extra $35 billion in economic activity to Metro Denver. Today the airport is one of the busiest in the country and the world, handling nearly 60 million passengers a year. The rapid growth in air traffic and more stringent security requirements have led to long delays at DIA in recent years, so a project to reconfigure the security checkpoints and open up the terminal was begun in 2018 to relieve this problem. Once completed in 2023, DIA will be able to handle 90 million passengers per year.

Tip #123: The main drawback to DIA is that it's 23 miles from downtown Denver, which can make ground transportation rather expensive.

Taxi and Uber rides can run upwards of $50, so take the ALine light rail to downtown to save money. It costs only $10.50, takes about 35 minutes, and goes directly to Union Station. Visit this webpage for rider information: https://www.rtd-denver.com/services/rail.

Chapter Review

The east side of Denver, comprising the eastern part of the City of Denver, Aurora, Commerce City, and points east, has quite a lot to offer Denverites. Beyond the popular attractions of Cheesman Park, City Park, and the East Colfax Corridor, even many locals don't venture farther east (except to go to the airport). But they are missing out.

Here's a summary of what we covered in Chapter 7 about the east side of Denver:

- In **East Denver**, Cheesman Park is a former cemetery that is now one of the city's most inviting and relaxing parks. Next door to Cheesman is the hugely popular Denver Botanic Gardens, one of the most renowned botanical gardens in the country. Farther east on Colfax Avenue are more Denver cultural institutions like the Sie FilmCenter, Tattered Cover Book Store, Twist & Shout Records, and the Bluebird Theater, a historic and intimate music venue. City Park has the Denver Zoo and Gates Planetarium, and on the eastern edge of Denver is the impressive Wings Over the Rockies Air & Space Museum.
- **Farther east and northeast** is the Stanley Marketplace, a multitenant market with popular eateries and boutique shops. Commerce City is the home of the Colorado Rapids professional soccer team at Dick's Sporting Goods Park. Nearby is the Rocky Mountain Arsenal National Wildlife Refuge, with more than 300 species of wildlife. Still farther east is the luxurious Gaylord Rockies Resort with its water park and stunning views of the mountains. Finally, on the northeastern edge of the metro area is DIA and its Jeppesen Terminal, whose white-peaked roof has become a symbol of Denver.

Chapter 8: Experience Denver Like a Local – North Side

Overview

This chapter will cover north-central Denver and the northern suburbs of Thornton, Northglenn, Federal Heights, Westminster, and Broomfield. The northern suburbs overlap with Adams County on the east and Jefferson County on the west. Stuck in a no man's land between Boulder, Weld, Adams, and Jefferson Counties, Broomfield decided to become its own county in 2001. I-25 and the Boulder Turnpike (U.S. Highway 36) have long been the main transportation corridors and catalysts for growth on the north side of the metro area. In recent years, however, the completion of the E-470 toll road between I-76 and U.S. 36 has fueled even more suburban growth on Denver's northern fringe. Meanwhile, the 2020 opening of the light rail N (North) Line from Union Station to 124th Avenue in Thornton aims to reduce traffic on heavily congested I-25.

North Denver

How locals define "North Denver" really depends on who you talk to. Some long-time residents refer to the neighborhoods directly northwest of downtown as "North Denver" or "Northside," but most call this area "Northwest Denver." For our purposes, we'll focus on north-central Denver, which is centered on the intersection of I-70 and I-25 (some Denverites will remember this intersection was once called the "Mousetrap" because of the way the tangled overpasses looked from the air). This area includes the neighborhood of Globeville and some attractions north of the RiNo District.

National Western Stock Show

4655 Humboldt St., Denver

Nothing says "Denver" like the National Western Stock Show, the world's largest livestock exhibition, farm animals, equestrian events, and rodeos. It's held over 16 days in January at the National Western Complex at I-70 and Brighton Boulevard. The stock show started in 1906 as a way to demonstrate better breeding and feeding techniques to Western stockmen. However, it soon expanded to welcome participants from around the world. In 1925, the agricultural youth organization 4-H began taking part, and in 1931, a rodeo competition was added. I remember taking several school field trips there, and as a city kid, the intense smells of cattle and horses were quite the shock!

Today, the stock show is perhaps best known for its many large horse shows, which draw close to 20,000 entrants per year with events like Hunters & Jumpers and the Draft Horse Show & Pull. But there's nothing quite like the excitement of the bronco buster rodeos when rodeo champions from all over the world come to compete. Other fun events include the Mexican Rodeo Extravaganza, which features Mexican-style bull riding, trick roping, mariachi music, and Portuguese-style bullfights (in which bulls are <u>not</u> killed). Many of the events take place at the nearby Denver Coliseum, on the south side of I-70. Visit the stock show's website for the full schedule of events and tickets: https://nationalwestern.com/.

In 2015, Denver unveiled a plan to redevelop and expand the 600,000-square-foot National Western Complex into the 2.2-million-square-foot "National Western Center." The plan includes the construction of 20 acres of plazas and community meeting spaces, research labs, new stockyards, and a new headquarters building for the Western Stock Show Association, which operates the stock show. But, perhaps as a sign of Denver's growing distance from its agricultural roots, voters in 2021 turned down public funding for a new arena and public market on the expanded site. However, construction continues on other parts of the project and is due to be completed in 2023.

Tip #124: Keep your eyes peeled for the National Western Stock Show's Kick-Off Parade, held downtown to open the stock show.

It features a grand marshal ushering 30 long-horn steers along the length of 17th Street from Union Station to the Brown Palace Hotel, which traditionally buys the biggest steer for display in its lobby during the stock show! Go to this webpage for more information: https://nationalwestern.com/special-events/parade/.

Forney Transportation Museum

4303 Brighton Blvd., Denver

The 70,000-square-foot Forney Transportation Museum is one of the finest transportation museums in the country. The museum showcases "anything on wheels," including Amelia Earhart's 1923 "Gold Bug" Kissel automobile, a Big Boy Union Pacific locomotive–the largest steam locomotive ever built–an 1888 Denver cable car, and more than 800 other transportation artifacts.

The museum started in the 1950s as the private antique car collection of J.D. Forney, the founder of Forney Industries, a Fort Collins manufacturer of soldering irons and welding equipment. When he started to run out of space for his ever-growing collection, he built a new building in Fort Collins and officially founded the museum in 1961. Unfortunately, the museum soon ran out of space again and, in 1968, relocated to the old Tramway Powerhouse in Denver. That 1901 building proved costly to maintain, and Forney sold it to REI for its flagship store. In 1999, the museum moved into a newer warehouse building, where it's still located today. For anyone interested in antique cars, locomotives, or airplanes, the Forney Transportation Museum is a must-see.

Globeville

Bounded by 52nd Ave., Inca St., and the South Platte River, Denver

Globeville has long been Denver's neighborhood of industry and the immigrants who worked in its factories. In the 1880s, the Globe Smelting & Refining plant became a magnet for a new neighborhood that housed thousands of immigrants from central, northern, and eastern Europe working at the facility. The separate town of Globeville was founded in 1891 and then annexed by Denver in 1902. Other smelters, railroad facilities, and packing plants emerged, but so did many churches catering to specific immigrant communities; the churches still dot the neighborhood today.

From the beginning, Globeville has been largely cut off from the rest of the city by the South Platte and surrounding railroad tracks. The neighborhood became even more isolated when the construction of I-25 and I-70 in the mid-20th century divided the neighborhood into quadrants. In the late 20th century, early immigrant families largely moved out, and Hispanic and Latino families moved in. Today, Hispanics make up 90% of Globeville's residents.

That said, the Globe Hall music venue (4483 Logan St.) builds on Globeville's diverse roots with indie rock, bluegrass, and country music acts from around the country. The cozy, standing-room general admission space, coupled with its scrumptious Texas-style barbecue and local craft beers, gives Globe Hall an "intimate saloon" feel. It's a fun place to get exposure to some new music while enjoying barbecue sandwiches and brisket! Visit their website for upcoming performances: https://globehall.com/.

Northern Suburbs

The northern suburbs of Denver, including Thornton, Northglenn, Federal Heights, Westminster, and Broomfield, were the last metro areas to see major growth. Westminster started as a small farming community in the 1880s and grew very slowly until the 1950s, when suburban growth started to take off. Thornton and Northglenn were founded in the 1950s as master-planned communities, and

Broomfield wasn't incorporated until 1961. Today, Westminster and Thornton each have more than 100,000 people, and Broomfield is fast approaching that size with 75,000 people. Broomfield, in particular, has attracted a lot of high-tech companies, giving the Denver Tech Center on the south side of the metro area a run for its money.

Water World

8801 N. Pecos St., Federal Heights

One of the highlights of my summers growing up in Denver was a trip to Water World in Federal Heights. I loved spending all day going down the impossibly high water slides and riding the waves in the giant wave pool–it was the closest thing we had to an ocean in Colorado. Water World, operated by the Hyland Hills Park & Recreation District, first opened in 1979 and has expanded many times since then. With 52 water rides and features covering 70 acres, Water World is one of the largest and best-rated water parks in the country.

Today, the outdoor water park has two wave pools, including the original Thunder Bay. One of the most popular attractions is the dinosaur-themed Journey to the Center of the Earth, which takes guests on rafts on a five-minute ride down chutes and through caverns. The Screamin' Mimi truly gets thrill-seekers screaming when they ride boards down a type of roller coaster at 30 mph and skip across the water in the pool at the bottom. Recently added is the Colorado-themed Alpine Springs park-within-a-park connected to the rest of Water World by a gondola. With so many rides suited for people of all ages and levels of daring, families can spend all day here having a blast. Visit the park's website for more information and tickets: https://www.waterworldcolorado.com/.

Tip #125: On a cool and rainy day, check the park's website to ensure it's open.

Water World is generally open Memorial Day through Labor Day weekends. Still, if the weather is cool, rainy, or stormy–which often happens in early summer—the park will be closed for "guest comfort and safety." Water World is entirely outdoors, after all!

Westminster Castle

3455 W. 83rd Ave., Westminster

Probably the most imposing historical landmark in the northern suburbs is Westminster Castle, a giant sandstone structure that dominates a hill with fantastic views of Denver and the Front Range. The "castle" was actually the main building for the now-defunct Westminster University. The Romanesque building was completed in 1893, but due to economic problems, the university didn't open until 1908. The school was hit with even more problems in 1917 when most of the student body was sent to Europe to fight in World War I; the university never fully recovered. A Christian group called Pillar of Fire took over the campus in 1920 and started their own school called Westminster College and eventually changed the name to Belleview College. The college no longer exists, but Pillar of Fire still operates a K-12 school on-site.

Today, locals often call the building the "Pillar of Fire," not just for the church that owns it but for its deep red sandstone exterior and the 175-foot tower that lights up as the sun goes down. Unfortunately, there are no public tours of Westminster Castle, but it's worth driving by to see this magnificent structure and the unparalleled views of Denver to the south and the Front Range to the west. The Castle is on the National Register of Historic Places.

Adventure Golf & Raceway

9650 N. Sheridan Blvd., Westminster

There are many miniature golf courses in the Denver area, but none are more interesting or fun than Adventure Golf & Raceway, which is like a small amusement park with mini-golf, go-karts, bumper cars, a ropes course, and a maze. The beautifully landscaped park has three 18-hole mini-golf courses, including the Lost Continent, Adventure Cove, and Buccaneer Bay. Those 16 and up can drive a well-powered electric go-kart around the short raceway. If you like to crash, you can try bumper cars. People with a tolerance for heights can test their balance by walking tightropes, balance beams, and barrels suspended 25 feet in the air (with a safety harness on, of course). Below is a two-level maze that will challenge anyone's sense of direction. In other words, there's plenty at Adventure Golf & Raceway to keep the whole family busy for a day! Go to their website for visitor information: https://www.adventuregolfandraceway.com/.

Tip #126: If real golf is your thing, you're in luck. You can drop the kids off at Adventure Golf & Raceway and play a round at the championship-level Greg Mastriona Golf Courses next door.

They include an 18-hole course, a 9-hole course, and a driving range. There's also an Italian restaurant in the clubhouse. Visit this website for more information: https://www.golfhylandhills.com/.

Butterfly Pavilion

6252 W. 104th Ave., Westminster

The Butterfly Pavilion is a conservatory for over 1,500 species of butterflies and other insects and invertebrates. It opened in 1995 as the first stand-alone nonprofit insect zoo in the United States. The 30,000-square-foot facility has five exhibits, the largest being the Wings of the Tropics, featuring 1,200 free-flying butterflies and 200 tropical plant species. Other exhibits include Water's Edge, which highlights sea stars, sea cucumbers, and other invertebrates of tide pools, and Crawl-A-See-Em, which has pettable tarantulas for the brave. The newest exhibit, Colorado Backyard, showcases local insects like ladybugs. There's also a half-mile-long trail outside where visitors can see insects in their natural environment.

The Butterfly Pavilion is not just a zoo but an educational institution that offers programs to educate the public on the importance of insects. Daily programs include feeding demonstrations, guided tours, and interactive presentations. In addition, special events like the Beekeeping Bootcamp, macro photography classes, and pollinator programs bring guests even closer to nature. The Butterfly Pavilion is truly a one-of-a-kind experience that the whole family will enjoy and learn from. Explore their website to learn more: https://butterflies.org/.

Tip #127: If you didn't get enough butterflies at the Butterfly Pavilion, check out Butterflies at Chatfield Farms, an exhibit created every summer by the Butterfly Pavilion at the Denver Botanic Gardens' Chatfield Farms' native plant refuge.

The seasonal butterfly house showcases hundreds of butterflies and 50 plant species native to Colorado. See this webpage to plan your visit: https://butterflies.org/exhibit/offsite-exhibits/.

Chapter Review

In this chapter, we covered the north side of Metro Denver, including north-central Denver and the northern suburbs of Thornton, Northglenn, Federal Heights, Westminster, and Broomfield. North-central Denver is centered on Globeville, a once-industrial neighborhood that was home to many immigrant families working in its factories. The northern suburbs remained mostly farmland into the mid-20th century, when suburban growth took off in a big way. Today, the north side is home to some of the most interesting and fun attractions in Metro Denver.

Here's a summary of what we covered in Chapter 8:

- In **North Denver**, the National Western Stock Show showcases Denver's Western roots with the country's largest exhibition of livestock, horse shows, and rodeos. The Forney Transportation Museum has one of the country's largest collections of "anything on two wheels," including antique cars, locomotives, and airplanes. The neighborhood of Globeville has a great diversity of churches, and the Globe Hall music venue brings to life Denver's diverse music scene.

- The **northern suburbs** draw summer fun-seekers to places like Water World, one of the country's largest and best-rated water parks, and Adventure Golf & Raceway, the Denver area's largest and most interesting miniature golf course. The Westminster Castle amazes architecture fans and history buffs, while the Butterfly Pavilion, the first stand-alone insect zoo in the U.S., delights nature lovers with its huge collection of butterflies and other insects and invertebrates.

Chapter 9: Frequently Asked Questions (FAQs)

This chapter serves as a general guide on visiting and living in Denver. In the FAQs, we cover topics like the best time of year to visit, Denver's climate, free things to do, and good activities for kids. You'll find that there is no shortage of things to see and do in Denver for people of every age and interest.

Frequently Asked Questions (FAQs)

- What's the best time of year to visit Denver?

The answer to this question depends on what you like to do. Denver is a magnet for lovers of the outdoors in all seasons, but the summer and fall offer the best opportunities for hiking, biking, boating, kayaking, and camping. Outdoor festivals and concerts abound in the summer as well. Winter is best suited for indoor activities and visiting the city's many cultural and gastronomic destinations. Many skiers passing through Denver on their way to Colorado's world-class ski resorts can stop in Denver for a few days to experience some of these attractions.

- What's the weather like in Denver?

The best way to describe Denver's weather is "highly variable." Denver experiences all four seasons, but often in the same month and sometimes in the same week. As a result, the city can experience wild weather swings in the spring and fall, going from hot and sunny one day to cold and snowy the next. Winters tend to be cold and dry, but even days in the 60s are not uncommon. Spring and early summer are usually the wettest and stormiest times of the year, but thunderstorms and snowstorms can occur almost any time of year (July and August are the only reliably snow-free months). Summers are seeing more blistering heat waves, but even cool and rainy days are not out of the question. In short, the best thing to do is check the forecast and plan to dress in layers.

Denver's semi-arid climate averages about 14.5 inches of precipitation per year. A lot of this falls in the form of snow from October to May and averages about 50 inches per year. The best part of Denver's weather, in my opinion, is the regular sunshine. Denver averages more than 300 sunny days per year.

- What are some free/cheap things to do in Denver?

First and foremost are the many hiking and biking trails and parks throughout Denver. The Cherry Creek and South Platte River Trails alone offer 76 miles of biking bliss and intersect in Riverfront Park. City Park, Sloan's Lake Park, Washington Park, and Cheesman Park are great places to stroll easy trails or take a leisurely boat ride around a lake. North Table Mountain Park and Roxborough State Park in Jefferson County have some vigorous trails that reward hikers with stunning views of the city.

Art lovers can walk the streets of the RiNo District to see more than 70 small-to-giant-size murals adorning the sides of buildings; the RiNo Art Alley has the greatest concentration of murals. For the cost of a light rail ticket, art aficionados can also take the W (West) Line from downtown to Lakewood and admire some impressive, locally-created artworks at each station. There are also many free cultural festivals and events throughout the year, like the Five Points Jazz Festival in the Five Points neighborhood (June), the Colorado Dragon Boat Festival in Sloan's Lake Park (July), First Fridays at the Art District on Santa Fe (every month), and the Friday Night Bazaar in the RiNo District (every Friday in summer).

- What are the most unique things to do in Denver?

Although Denver has become a modern, cosmopolitan metropolis, it's still possible to explore the Western roots that make it unique. Inside a re-creation of Bent's Old Fort in Morrison, the Fort restaurant offers Rocky Mountain cuisine that evokes the old frontier. The Buckhorn Exchange is Denver's oldest restaurant, and its bison steaks and taxidermied walls won't let you forget you're out West. Outdoor adventurers can kayak down man-made chutes in LoDo's Confluence Park or Clear Creek White Water Park in Golden.

Upper Downtown's American Museum of Western Art celebrates Western artists like Russell and Remington, whose artwork memorably captures the Old West. The American Mountaineering Museum in Golden offers a one-of-a-kind exploration of the challenges of mountaineering, a favorite Colorado pastime. You can soak in late-19th century elegance and history with afternoon high tea at the Brown Palace Hotel. Finally, nothing says "Denver" like attending the National Western Stock Show in January.

- What are some fun activities for kids in Denver?

There's no shortage of fun things to keep kids busy in Metro Denver. The Denver Zoo in City Park is one of the best in the country and offers many programs and events aimed at the younger set. The nearby Denver Museum of Nature & Science, with its world-class dinosaur exhibits, is a kid favorite, and the star shows in its Gates Planetarium will awe them even more. Dinosaur lovers will also get a kick out of the dinosaur fossils they'll find at Dinosaur Ridge near Morrison. Kids marvel at the Downtown Aquarium's large collection of sea and river life. Children enamored with trains and cars will love the Forney Transportation Museum near downtown and the Colorado Railroad Museum in Golden, where they can ride real trains. Most kids will be delighted when butterflies land on them at the Butterfly Pavilion in Westminster, or they get a chance to pet goats and other farm animals at the Four Mile Historic Park near Glendale.

Of course, summer would not be complete without a few trips to an amusement park. Elitch Gardens in LoDo is the state's largest, with many thrilling rides. Lakeside Amusement Park is a throwback to the old-timey parks of the early 20th century and has a miniature train that goes around Lake Rhoda. Water World in Federal Heights is one of the largest water parks in the country and has 52 water rides and features, including impossibly high water slides and two giant wave pools.

- Is Denver LGBTQ+ friendly?

Denver is very gay-friendly, with the largest LGBTQ+ community between Chicago and the West Coast. In fact, it has one of the largest Pride events in the country in June, with a massive parade and events throughout the city. Denver also boasts a large number of gay bars and nightclubs that are usually packed on weekends. Gay couples will feel at ease in most of Denver's welcoming neighborhoods, and the general friendliness of Denverites will make singles feel at home, too, no matter where they go in the metro area.

About the Author

Todd Faulk was born and raised in Denver, Colorado, and obtained his undergraduate degree from the University of Colorado at Denver. He has since made frequent visits to the city to see family and friends. In addition, Mr. Faulk is a professional travel writer, history buff, and avid world traveler. He has visited all 50 U.S. states and 70 countries and loves exploring and experiencing places as locals do. Returning to Denver for several extended visits in the last few years has given Mr. Faulk a fresh view of his hometown, which he enjoys sharing with anyone interested in coming to the Mile High City.

HowExpert publishes how to guides by everyday experts. Visit HowExpert.com to learn more.

Recommended Resources

- HowExpert.com – How To Guides by Everyday Experts.
- HowExpert.com/free – Free HowExpert Email Newsletter.
- HowExpert.com/books – HowExpert Books
- HowExpert.com/courses – HowExpert Courses
- HowExpert.com/clothing – HowExpert Clothing
- HowExpert.com/membership – HowExpert Membership Site
- HowExpert.com/affiliates – HowExpert Affiliate Program
- HowExpert.com/jobs – HowExpert Jobs
- HowExpert.com/writers – Write About Your #1 Passion/Knowledge/Expertise & Become a HowExpert Author.
- HowExpert.com/resources – Additional HowExpert Recommended Resources
- YouTube.com/HowExpert – Subscribe to HowExpert YouTube.
- Instagram.com/HowExpert – Follow HowExpert on Instagram.
- Facebook.com/HowExpert – Follow HowExpert on Facebook.
- TikTok.com/@HowExpert – Follow HowExpert on TikTok.